FIRST

LOVE

KIRSTON JOHNSON

ISBN 978-0-578-46470-1 (paperback Edition)

Dedication

This book is dedicated to every girl or woman who is single or has been single. It is to the beautiful ladies who have struggled in their singleness, who have felt lonely, rejected or abandoned. My prayer is that through these pages of my own journey you will learn from my mistakes, and be encouraged and inspired by where God has taken me through my own heartaches and heartbreaks.

A special dedication to all my friends who have walked out my single season with me and continue to do so. This is a compilation of the many girl talks we have shared throughout our years together. I am so thankful I have had loyal friends who have seen me through some very tough times.

I am thankful and honored to have written this book. God planted the seed in my heart awhile ago, and it has taken me time, strength, and courage to finish it. I hope that these are not just words on a page, but I hope that they strike your heart and give you permission to feel what you need to and be healed in the process. All glory to God, the *First Love* of my life, who has loved me unconditionally and relentlessly.

Table of Contents

Introduction

I am single and have been my whole life. I am twenty-five years old at the start of writing this. Not even having a middle school relationship that lasted a day or a week like most can say they've had. From the time I was a child I have been a hopeless romantic. I had an idea of what a relationship should look like, and I never settled. Some may think this is a noble thing, others may think it pathetic, but no matter what your opinion is, give me a chance to share my story before you make your consensus.

I grew up in Orange County, California where dreams were made and money was plenty. Growing up I was well off. My dad was a workaholic with a drinking problem and my mom was codependent. My parents fought constantly and didn't show the best picture of marriage. They separated when I moved away to college in 2008 and finalized their divorce just this year in 2013. Many would think that this would scare me from getting married, but for some reason it has always motivated me. It has motivated me to want to do things the right way because I already knew how to do things the wrong way. Like I said, I am a hopeless romantic.

I just knew from early on what God intended it to be like. Marriage is supposed to be filled with unconditional love that encourages and supports you to be the very best version of yourself and is God centered. Man and wife are to complete the image of God, his masculine and feminine side. It is intended to be a heavenly pairing of two people who complement each other so well, not that they complete each other, but that they highlight the strengths of one another. They balance the flaws in each other with the perfect mixture of grace and truth. Grace gives the truth a sweeter aftertaste than just by itself.

Marriage should be filled with hopes, dreams, empowerment, security, and happiness. This is how God intended it. But because of the ways of our world, it seems as if it is impossible to have those things describe a marriage these days. Instead many people think of divorce when they hear the word marriage. With the statistics getting higher and higher in the rate of divorce, separations, and broken families, it is no wonder some people opt out of it altogether and live a life filled with different partners or lovers.

But the good news is, it is possible. Not that I have experienced it yet, but there are many stories of happily married people who run into life's issues and come out on the other side of them not only okay, but on top. But this book is not about marriage, it is about the before marriage: the single life.

Through these pages I will be discussing my experience as a single girl living in a "Christian world," aka church bubble, as well as my experiences before I started following Jesus. I will not only discuss my experiences, but the experiences of some of my also single friends. My views and take on the subject are just my personal thoughts and feelings and what I have found to be true for myself. There is no formula to living out a single life while looking for a man. This book is not to just whine and complain about singlehood, but it is to learn to embrace it in the long waiting.

Your love story is right around the corner whether you believe it or not. Better to believe it and have hope rather than to pity yourself and be miserable during this season of your life. You only get it once, and it is such a small portion of your life, so why not celebrate it, live life to its fullest and encourage others to do the same in the meantime.

1.

Fairytale or Future?

I remember daydreaming of the man I would marry, my wedding, our children and life together. I had always been so hopeful yet a hopeless romantic. I love *love*, and I still believe there is a 'happy ever after' story for me. But as life goes on, I have become more and more jaded in regards to the guys around me. The single guys that are afraid to commit, so they tell you what you want to hear in order to string you along, long enough for them to get what they want from you.

All I want is to love someone and be loved. I want them to want to be with me, spend time with me, and have eyes for only me. I never knew it would be so hard to find that. Then as a Christian, you want a guy who reads his Bible and actually prays. In my experience, guys like that have been few and far between in church life. It's not that only the guys in church are not up to par with where you would like them to be. There are many girls as well, but for this case I am just talking about the search for a man of God in a church world that is filled with guys who depend on their own strength to get them through. They discredit God's hand in their life and are too prideful to ask for help. And if these guys cannot ask God for help and be in a relationship with Him, how will they ever be in a relationship with a girl like me?

I read my bible, I pray, but besides doing the things we are "supposed to," I love Jesus with all my heart. I want to follow Him and make Him proud. And if I am going to be with someone, he needs to have that same heart. But for some reason, (1) I do not find many single guys like that and (2) I hold onto a glimmer of hope that one of these guys will actually get it together and realize who God is and then they could see whom I am.

Right now, at this point in my life, I wonder what I am doing and what I am supposed to do. It is so hard to wait around for this *Prince Charming* to show up when I am starting to wonder if he even exists. I want to wait well and be pure and have the right attitude. But more and more, I am finding it harder to do that. I think I just never expected finding him to take this long. I wasn't ready for everyone else around me to get engaged, married, and have babies while I am still single and nowhere near joining them. No one prepares you for that. I guess that is why I am writing this book. I want those single girls to know that they are not alone, and it is hard. But there is definitely light at the end of the tunnel. I know there is! I haven't experienced it yet, but I know God is faithful and He delivers on His promises. It seems as if the books that I have read about love, relationships, and singleness have all been so one-sided. It usually is in the perspective of after being married and talking about *when* they were single. So I thought it would be best to write something about the processes from single life to love life to finally reach married life. So here we are in the single life...

But as of right now, don't be discouraged. Dream about your *happily ever after* and your future with the man of your dreams because it will happen, you just have to believe. That is what faith is, believing without seeing and without ceasing until you see it come to pass. It's hard; it's not going to be easy, but it will be worth it.

Happily Ever After

I am learning that happily ever after comes before your "*Happily Ever After*." I have realized that when I am happy the things I actually want or the life that I want is more attracted to me. Happy, to me, means that I am where I am supposed to be and I am doing what I am supposed to be doing. It is a weird paradox because how do you know you are doing what you are supposed to be doing? Living by your morals and values and being true to yourself comes from doing what you are supposed to be doing. But I guess what I am trying to say is that when we are following God, obeying Him, and listening to the Holy Spirit is when we are doing what we are meant to be doing. Therefore, we can be happy. And when we are happy, we are ourselves and people are more attracted to us. When we are doing the things we are passionate about, when we trust God and His plan, and when we are focusing more on Him and not ourselves, that is when "all these things will be added" to us.

I am currently twenty-five years old, still single, and living in Australia. I felt called to move here for leadership college with a focus in Ministry. Before I came here, things were not going well for me. I was not happy, and I was not living how I knew I was meant to. But as soon as I obeyed God and moved here, everything just clicked. Now I know this could look as if I were running away from my problems back home, but I felt peace about that not being the case before I left. But what is interesting is how much things have changed for me for the better ever since. Since I am more myself, I am definitely getting more attention and interest from guys. I am not saying this to boast, I just find it interesting that because I am happy and happy with myself, people, guys specifically are drawn to me. This isn't some new concept that you have never heard before. We all know that until we accept ourselves, no one else can. But I want to remind you and encourage you of this key point: to be happy with yourself and love yourself before you let anyone else.

In the past I found this to be quite hard and frustrating at times because I knew it, but I couldn't do it. I didn't like who I was. But now I am realizing that I don't have to be perfect. I make mistakes all the time. But God's grace is enough. His grace makes me beautiful inside and out. His grace is what makes me happy. When we lean on God's grace, nothing can bring us down or take us out. When we are in God's grace zone that is what sets us up and sets us apart to be where we really ought to be. How we can get in God's grace zone is by obeying him. I am not just talking about obeying the obvious or obeying in the things that we struggle with, but we must obey Him in the things He is calling us to. And being in the grace zone does not mean everything will be perfect and you won't still make mistakes. You may fall while in the grace zone, but there is grace there to catch you and help you back up. That is the grace zone, accepting God's mercy and love even when you may fall back into old ways that have tried to hold you back in the past.

Right before I moved to Australia, I was involved with a guy who I had a very unhealthy relationship with. We were very physical, and I let him treat me in devaluing ways. But I let him. What I am learning is that I must take responsibility for my actions or else I could repeat the past mistakes. He was at fault as well in many ways, but ultimately I let him. This is not to guilt or shame myself at all. I do not feel condemned for my past actions, but I did and do feel convicted by the mistakes that I made. All God really cares about and all that really matters is what I do with it. So if I take responsibility now, ask for forgiveness, forgive him and myself, and then let it go, I can move on and not have to look back. Dwelling on the things of the past only help us repeat the past. But when we truly know the truth of the situation and how much God really loves us, we won't make the same mistakes.

Happily ever after to me is living how I want to live now, with or without a boyfriend or husband. Being happy does not come from your marital status or how you look, but it comes from a decision. Make a decision to obey God, let things go, and take responsibility of your actions. Take initiative for your own life and don't just wait around for things to change. God wants to change your life, but He can only do so when you take a step forward in what He is calling you to and that is what obedience looks like.

2.

The Meantime

The meantime is the waiting period of life, which, if you haven't already noticed, is how the majority of life is spent. Waiting can be a drag if we let it or we can choose to make it enjoyable! Even once the waiting is over, there is always something else to wait for after that. We are human beings who are always looking to what is next. And if we aren't careful, we can easily waste our lives away by always looking to what is ahead rather than focusing on what is right in front of us. Life is too good to waste your time not waiting well, and God is far too great. You might ask yourself *what does waiting well look like?* Waiting well looks like you living your life fully: dreaming, doing, and going! Have dreams for your life and accomplish them. And if you want to go and move somewhere new and different or if you want to travel, then do it! This is the best time to do it, while you are single and in waiting.

There are many benefits to being single. Being single means you have no strings attached. You have fewer responsibilities, and you really only need to look after yourself. If it is a career you want or if it is going to school, then do that. At the end of the day, life is short, and if you are waiting around to get married and have kids, then you are missing an opportunity and gift that God is giving you - your days of singleness. Singleness is not very long when you look at the whole span of life and how long you will actually be married, 'Till' death do you part.'

I know it can be frustrating in the waiting, believe me I understand. But if we can remind ourselves to put things into perspective, encourage ourselves to be bold and brave in our waiting, and dare to be the women we desire to be, waiting can become a lot less like waiting and a lot more like living.

Live the life you were meant to live. *Life is meant-to-be enjoyed not endured.* We may have to wait for certain things like having children, but you can still have a family while single. It will just consist more of friends than biological children. Or become a spiritual mother to some youth who are in need of guidance like you were. I believe there are so many missed opportunities that could make an impact on our lives and our futures if we would open our eyes and look at our lives for what they are rather than what they aren't...yet!

Being single is actually a gift. I remember people would say that to me or I would read books that explained it that way, and I thought *of course they would say that now that they are married.* But at this point in my journey, I am really beginning to believe that, and I am not even married yet. I think it is important for us to understand this now while we are still single because it will make this time even more enjoyable.

Singleness doesn't have to have the stigma around it that the world tries to portray it as. It does not have to be you at home alone on a Friday night in pjs, eating ice cream while crying to a chick flick. But it also can be. I have found satisfaction in nights like that or going out for a night on the town. I am content doing both, and I don't wallow in self-pity when I have nothing to do and no one to do it with. But I did have times like that when I felt so miserable and lonely. When I have felt hopeless and less than because I didn't have a boyfriend. I have felt the tortured, agonizing pain of being single where everyone around me seemed to have someone. I spent years like this until I realized it was time to put on my "big girl pants" as my friend likes to say and start living my life. There are still times when my *woe-is-me* mentality likes to creep in from time to time, but I am learning to do that less and less and start living more and more.

Living life does not always look like walks on the beach and buying an expensive handbag. It is actually what is going on internally that dictates whether we are living to the best of our ability with what we have been given. Yes, it is nice to be able to buy what you want, and being single definitely gives you more freedom for that because you don't have someone checking on what you are spending. But are you at peace with who God has created you to be and the life He has given you thus far? Until we can get the revelation that we are blessed and are actually living an amazing life, He can't move us forward into bigger and better things. The more He gives us, the more responsibilities come with it. So until we live accordingly and let Him change our perspectives, He can't give us more. He will never give us more than we can handle.

This isn't to worry you or give you anxiety that you are living wrong or thinking wrong. It is to show you that we are all on a journey, and God knows what is best for us and when the timing is right. If you just trust Him, it will be much easier for you, and you will be able to live a life that is full rather than empty, whatever full looks like for you!

To Date or Not to Date?

To date or not to date has been a big question of mine for quite some time. Everyone is different in their approach to relationships.

Everyone who wants to get married has to ask him or herself that question. Do you decide not to date around and just wait for God to bring that perfect person for you? Or do you take initiative and put yourself out there, and along the way God will bring that person to you?

For me I have not been so sure of which is better. I have tried both, and still nothing has panned out yet in either approach. But what I can say is that whichever approach you choose, God will bring you that person when the time is right. So what do you do in the meantime? I have heard so many different stories from so many different people on when and how they met their spouse or significant other.

My friend Brittany, for instance, met her now husband just after getting out of a bad relationship. She did not want anything to do with guys or dating. She was over it. But then she met the man of her dreams. They began to spend time together, and eventually they became a couple and are now happily married with a baby.

On the other spectrum, there are so many marriages and relationships that happen off of dating websites and apps where you are actively seeking a relationship. One big dating pool filled with singles looking to fall in love. My mom met her boyfriend on a dating website and has been dating him for almost four years. With ever-increasing technological advances, our society and culture are changing the way single life and dating are experienced.

Now if we are just looking at how people meet and what the best way to meet someone is, I have found there is really no right or wrong way. But I do believe, as a woman of God, we are called to live out the single life in such a way that honors and trusts Him. Dating is a helpful tool to learn more about who you are and what you are looking for. It is up to you and what your convictions are on how you want to go about dating. Either way you will meet people you find attractive, possibly date them, and hopefully find someone you would love to share the rest of your life with.

But then there are those people who date just to date. They want the fun, no commitment; no strings attached type of relationships where nothing ever gets too serious or deep. I have actually seen this quite often in church life surprisingly, especially when it comes to guys. I think it is because they feel so much pressure from the get-go that they sabotage the relationship before it can even go anywhere. Some put these unrealistic, preconceived expectations on the dating relationship. They may feel the expectations and pressures from the girl or from family and friends as well as church leaders. Because the goal with dating, especially in church, is that there is intent to marry the person, which obviously is a good thing. But it can also destroy a relationship before it even starts if the person or couple is not secure enough to handle the pressure coming at them from all sides.

But then again, if it does not work out then it obviously was not meant to be. But it can cause so much heartbreak. It can also be awkward and uncomfortable circumstances for those involved when they do attend the same church and have the same group of friends, and of course I am speaking from personal experience. It is extremely difficult to see someone around who you had or still have feelings for. And also once that person starts dating other people, it can be even more painful.

I recently spoke with a coworker who is not a Christian about this specific topic, and it really does put into perspective how different the Christian community is when it comes to dating. Because we believe in waiting to have sex until married, living together before marriage is ruled out as well. For the world, this does not make sense. And logically it would make more sense to test things out before getting married, but that is where faith steps in. And if you are currently living with a boyfriend or sleeping with your boyfriend, believe me when I say there is no condemnation or judgment coming from me. I too have had my own experiences in the area of premarital sex. We all are on different journeys and have different convictions. We all have our weaknesses and struggles. But besides all of that, whether you are a Jesus follower or not, statistics prove that couples who live together before they get married are at a 33% higher risk than those who don't, to get divorced later on.

The single life is a time of growing pains, heartbreak, and navigating through it all one mountain at a time. People always tell me you will meet your husband when you least expect it, a saying that I have always hated. Only because I always want to meet that person and am looking to meet him, and I don't think I can ever stop that. I don't think I am just going to one day not think about it at all until I do meet and marry him. So to say I will least expect it is probably not completely true. I do, however, think I will meet him in the most random of ways or time of my life, so in that case I will least expect it. But honestly I have been expecting him ever since I can remember. I have always wanted to be married or looked forward to it since I was a child. I know I am strange, but there is just something about it. I just think we should all have a partner in life besides God to help us through the waves and windstorms, who can be by our side no matter what happens.

Waiting Well

In the meantime, while you wait you are going to be confronted with many temptations to compare yourself to others who are in relationships and married and the temptation to grow weary because of it. As more and more time goes on while you wait, more people around you will get married, more people around you will start having children, and it is so easy to compare and get jealous of others. It is easy to think, *why them* and *why not me*. It is easy to get angry and even take it out on others because of their fortune. I have had friends experience this, and I have been tempted myself. I have let others' happiness make me feel less happy because I have felt left behind and nowhere near where they are at in life. I have coveted others lives because of being unhappy in my own. I can still struggle with it, and I think it gets harder and harder the longer I wait.

But the good news is we do not have to let it dictate our single days or our futures for that matter. I have tried to make a point to always celebrate others' blessings and promises fulfilled as best as possible. I would put myself in their shoes and know that when my time comes around, I want them to be as excited for me as I am for them. It is a challenge at times, especially when more and more people get engaged and married. But their happiness does not take away from what is ahead for me. There is plenty of goodness to go around in the world, and God is in control of it all so we have nothing to worry about. The more we can celebrate with others, the more people will want you around and want you to be a part of their lives. And when your time comes, everything will already be set for you. You will have the community around you that you will need once you start a family with your future man.

Waiting well looks like not growing weary in your singleness. It is you pouring into others and not feeling sorry for yourself all the time. It is holding onto the promises of God and not swaying or settling for something less than what you know He has told you. It is not giving up or backing down in what you know to be true, no matter how many people want to give you advice on how to live out your singleness. People want you to be happy at the end of the day, and sometimes they think they know the answers for your life because they are no longer single. But they don't, and although they have good intentions, the only person you need to be listening to is the Holy Spirit. He will nudge you in the right directions in all areas of life, especially when it comes to your single season of life.

One of my biggest desires and goals was that I would do this single season well. I don't think I realized when I set out, how long it would take. Isn't that life with God though? We make these bold declarations in a moment, not foreseeing that this moment can last years and years. And that bold passion can slowly become harder and harder to keep aflame. But that is when courage comes in. I pray that all of us, no matter what season we are in, will be courageous in whatever we do. Let's not despise our declarations we make when we begin to grow a bit weary. Let us find rest in Jesus and remember that He is faithful in all things, specifically His promises to us!

3.

Is There Something Wrong with Me?

For the longest time, actually most of my adolescence and early adulthood, I really believed there was something wrong with me. I couldn't understand why I couldn't get a boyfriend. Most of my friends had boyfriends, multiple boyfriends in fact, and I hadn't even had one.

It took me a lot of struggling with the idea that there was something wrong with me before I really grasped why I hadn't had a boyfriend yet. God placed it in my heart at an early age that I wanted to be with the one I would marry. This gave me high expectations, mostly too high. I also had not been ready. Not that there was something wrong with me, but God knew I would not choose the right one, and He knew it was not my time. And since I am writing to you still single, it still is not the right time. But I have definitely realized that it is not because I am not pretty enough, skinny enough, smart enough, or funny enough. I now know that I am enough. Period.

Not feeling good enough is a common struggle for many people, guys and girls. I do think guys hide it better because most males, generally speaking, do not express their feelings as much as females do. This feeling and void of not being enough can cause many of life's issues. It can cause people to continuously try to prove something, give into something or someone, and if it isn't one thing it is another; whatever can fill that void is what people will resort to. People can live with the empty void their whole lives. It is easy to not be aware of it too, if you have lived with it long enough. That is why it is so important to seek God at all times.

I do find, at this point in my life, that God is teaching me how to trust Him. Until I can trust God and have that intimacy with Him, then I will not be able to do that with a man. I mean, seriously, if I can't trust God then I can't trust anyone. And God is also jealous for you and me. I never really understood what that meant, but now I get it. It is like when you like a guy, and there are all these girls trying to get his attention, and you just want him to pay attention to you and you only. God is the same way. He does not want to be fighting for our attention and love all the time. He does not want any guy taking His place in our hearts and lives because He is our creator. He knows us better than ourselves or anyone else. He does not want to play second string in our game of life. He is the star player ready to set us up for a win if we would just give him the ball.

God knows what He is doing, and He knows when the perfect time is for us to step into a relationship or not. But instead so many times we try to control things and do what we want because we think we know what is best. If that were the case, then we would not need God. And we never want to put a guy in God's place because (1) that would never work and (2) the right guy won't want that anyway. Until we let go of our preconceived ideas and what we think we want, God can't fulfill the promises He has made to us when it comes to a husband.

Rejection

Guys that don't do what they say they will do frustrate me the most. I have been involved with or dated guys who say one thing and do another; or say one thing and don't do it at all. I'm not sure which is worse. I recently went on a date with a guy, and it went really well...or at least I thought. The conversation was good, it was fun, and before it even ended he asked me to get lunch the following week. And now it has been over a week, and I haven't heard from him. It left me confused, frustrated, and to be completely honest...rejected. Rejection is the worst feeling to me and has also caused me much heartache and bad mistakes along the way.

Every time I have felt rejected I end up acting out, whether it be seeking attention from another guy or not having self-control in my anger. These issues have gotten much better throughout the years as I have gotten closer to God and know who I am and whose I am. But if I am not careful, it tends to creep up on me, and it can cause me to act in ways that I normally wouldn't. And then it brings me to this little pity party I have where I wish I had a boyfriend/husband so that I would not have to deal with this. Which I know will not solve anything for me, but it might make it easier.

I believe there are always issues and problems we have to face before God brings us the right person. But if we are not careful, it is easy to get caught up in focusing too much on the problems and why we are still single, when ultimately the answer lies within our relationship with God. That void in me that causes me to feel rejected is a void that only God can fix. God can only change the behavior that comes out of that feeling of rejection, once I allow Him to take over in that area. And for me to do that and surrender means I must fight my flesh, everything within me that wants to act out in my feelings, and not let those feelings get the best of me. As human beings we must be so aware of how we feel, why we feel that way, and then control our feelings as best as possible. We are called to not act out of our feelings with God's spirit of self-control guiding and helping us. This is not something we will ever master completely, but it is something that we must do if we want to live healthy, happy lives especially in relationships.

I think in the past Christians have felt that the need to control themselves means to repress themselves. This is where Christianity becomes religion rather than a relationship with God. It is where God becomes a tyrant rather than a Father. All God wants to do is love us and help us. But the world has made Him into something He isn't and has made it hard for us to accept His love and help. We are constantly trying to do things in our own strength and when we fail, we fall and fall hard. And when we do, He is right there to pick us up again. He is there to brush the dust off and make us clean again. No matter how many times we fall, He never gets tired of helping us back up.

Rejection may come from an even deeper place than a guy standing you up. Maybe you felt rejected by your parents. Maybe you were bullied at school. For whatever reason, I think it is safe to say that we have all felt the gut-wrenching despair of rejection. It not only takes over your heart with a deep pain, but it can cause our minds to spin out of control. It can send us into a bottomless pit of rejection after rejection with no end in sight. I eventually had to realize for myself that it wasn't the actual person or people who were rejecting me, but it was my mindset and perspective that caused me to feel rejected. I am not discounting anyone's feelings here; your feelings of rejection are real and valid. But feelings are fleeting and emotions can run wild when we let them. It is good to feel and have emotion, but when they rule your life is when it becomes a problem.

Once I let God into my hurt and rejection, He shed light on it for me. He showed me that it wasn't them actually rejecting me, but they weren't capable of loving me or treating me the way I expected them to. Hurt people hurt people. And when someone hasn't dealt with their own hurts and rejection they tend to reject and hurt others. I tended to attract the type of person who had been rejected too because I have a big heart and want to help, but in the process I just ended up heartbroken. This is why it is so important to know appropriate boundaries. You are only responsible for yourself at the end of the day, and how you treat people and let them treat you is on you. It is a harsh truth, but so freeing at the same time. When we realize that we are not responsible for others' actions it takes the burden off of us. Yes, we need to be there for people, but if we can't help ourselves first we are no use to them.

Love We Think We Deserve

"We accept the love we think we deserve."

I heard this quote once from the movie *The Perks of Being a Wallflower*. I remember sobbing during this movie because I realized how true that really is.

Proverbs 23:7a (NKJV):
7 For as he thinks in his heart, so is he.

What we believe about ourselves becomes the truth. The enemy will feed us lies if we allow him. That is why it is so important to know the truth. We must read our bibles, pray, and listen to the Holy Spirit and what He says about us. We must understand that we are a new creation. Because if we allow our past experiences, past mistakes and regrets to dictate our lives then we are nothing more than our past.

For me it has always been my relationships with boys or even just feelings for a boy that has been my kryptonite. The love and acceptance from a man who I care about is all I want. But for some reason, I always attracted and settled for the half menial attention from a boy who does not want to commit to being with me. When

I imagine someone who I care about actually loving me, treating me like a princess (how all girls should be treated), and wanting to be with me…it can scare me. Now why is that? Why are we afraid of the things we want the very most? It happens all the time. Some people even sabotage a relationship because it is going well. For me, I am afraid to be abandoned, leaving me broken and rejected. I am afraid to allow someone to love me because then there will be expectations of me and what if I disappoint? What if they get to know me better, and they find they don't actually love me at all? What if they meet someone better, prettier, funnier, smarter? The list goes on and on.

We all do this, don't we? We think of all the 'what ifs' in life and we worry that our worst nightmares will become reality. But if we sit back and let our fears smother us, we will never get anywhere. We will be paralyzed in our fear, resorting to unhealthy relationships that mask a void within our hearts that only God can fill. These fears not only keep us from a real, healthy, love-filled relationship with a man, but they can keep us from *the best love story ever told* with our Heavenly Father. Jesus is just waiting for us to let go of these fears and rest in Him. He is waiting for us to surrender to Him so that He can show us how much He truly cares. He has so many blessings, surprises, adventures that He wants to share with us. But instead, we resort to the belief that we do not deserve it (which we really don't), but God wants to give it to us anyway. I look back on all the mistakes I have made with boys, giving myself to these boys who don't truly care about me, and what does that say about myself? Because of my actions, I am basically telling them, "Hey, I don't care about myself, so you don't have to either. Do what you want with me, and I won't care." How sick is that? It blows my mind that some of us do this to ourselves. We are getting abused, and we just take it.

But Jesus didn't die for us to live this way. He did not care so much about us so that we would care little for ourselves. We are royalty. And we need to act like it. We need to rise above our past experiences and choose to live as the new creation God has called us to be. Royalty of the King should be our new stance. We wear invisible crowns that other's may not see at first, but the more often we put it on, the more visible it will become to others. And it won't be in a pretentious way, but in an authoritative, God-fearing way that is undeniable to those around us even if they don't fully see what it is we have on or understand what it is about us that makes us different from the rest of the world. This kind of attitude will attract the like, and he will be a God-fearing and loving man who will see your crown right away and treat you accordingly.

4.

Letting It Go

Someone once told me that I am still carrying around my dead weight from my past. I didn't understand it at first, what she meant by that. But then I finally understood. I was holding onto my past failures and mistakes while trying to live a better life. I hadn't let go of who I used to be, and it was causing me to act in ways that I once had. And as of right now, to be completely honest, I am not sure if I have fully let it go still. It all stems back to the idea of counterfeit love. I once lived a life where I was so afraid of having a real relationship that the only way I could get close to a male was by getting drunk and getting physical with him. My idea of love was so warped, but it was all I knew. I thought I had left that pattern I had once lived behind when I recommitted my life to Jesus and found a church and a new family there that I called home.

My life really started to take off, and I was so excited about it. I thought *finally I have arrived.* What a dangerous thought to have in the kingdom of God. That is one thing I have definitely learned and accepted, that we will never arrive, and there is always something to work on or work through with God. There is always more to learn and areas to grow in, but that is what is exciting about the Jesus-following life. God then brought someone into my "new" life whom brought up all those old habits and ways of thinking. He was the first guy I actually dated for more than two weeks. As soon as he ended things, without actually ending things (insert eye roll emoji), that's when I decided the only way I could get him back was to compromise myself and get more physical with him. Old habits die hard, as they say.

Of course, this did not work. After a long, dragged out, heartbreak after heartbreak I had to make a change. So once again, I had to make the decision to let go and let God have control over this area of my life. I had to decide. Do I want what I have always known or do I want the unknown that God is always calling us to? The unknown of where my future is headed. It was so scary, but I knew it would be worth it. Until we stop holding onto the things of our past, God can't do the work He wants to do. It is a painful process that only He can bring us through. It is a long process that continues all throughout our lives. But if we continue to move forward and keep giving it up to God, He will do what it takes to bring us to what He has called us to. God does not want us to keep looking back. He does not want us to keep living how we used to. But He can't do anything about it until we make the decision to leave it all behind.

Letting Go Isn't Easy

There have been various times in my life when I have decided to let go, and I can still remember the pain and sorrow. Letting go isn't always easy; it is one of the hardest things for us as humans to do. Some people choose to never let go, and it affects the momentum of their lives forever. It can keep them paralyzed with fear and moving forward, forcing them to face all the pain and sorrow and let God heal their heart which is never comfortable or easy. I know too many people who struggle with exactly that. They are afraid to let go of their past, and it keeps them right where they are. They are miserable and frustrated, but slowly that becomes who they are, if they let it.

It is sad to think of all the potential we have within us that does not come out because of fear; fear of the unknown. We would rather be miserable in our old ways because it is what we have always known. Our misery is safe. But God has called us to so much more than that. I think so many of us tend to forget that. We have different life experiences that take place and can either encourage us or debilitate us. Along the way, we can choose the beliefs they cause us to form or we can renounce them. We must renounce them if we want to grab hold of all God has planned for us. All the blessings He wants to give us are on the other side of decisions we make about our beliefs. Our beliefs are what cause us to act and behave in certain ways. Our behaviors shape and form our life. We are human, and self-control tends to be our biggest downfall. We try to do the right thing, but we are not always strong enough or capable of not making mistakes; because we are imperfect.

It is like Paul speaking in Romans 7: 14-25 (NLT):

"So the trouble is not with the law, for it is spiritual and good. The trouble is with me, for I am all too human, a slave to sin. I don't really understand myself, for I want to do what is right, but I don't do it. Instead, I do what I hate. But if I know that what I am doing is wrong, this shows that I agree that the law is good. So I am not the one doing wrong; it is sin living in me that does it.

And I know that nothing good lives in me, that is, in my sinful nature. I want to do what is right, but I can't. I want to do what is good, but I don't. I don't want to do what is wrong, but I do it anyway. But if I do what I don't want to do, I am not really the one doing wrong; it is sin living in me that does it.

I have discovered this principle of life—that when I want to do what is right, I inevitably do what is wrong. I love God's law with all my heart. But there is another power within me that is at war with my mind. This power makes me a slave to the sin that is still within me. Oh, what a miserable person I am! Who will free me from this life that is dominated by sin and death? Thank God! The answer is in Jesus Christ our Lord. So you see how it is: In my mind I really want to obey God's law, but because of my sinful nature I am a slave to sin."

This is who we are. We are Paul struggling with the sin we are so susceptible to. I get so frustrated with myself, and I feel like I am going crazy at times, going over and over again the mistakes I make. My judgments of myself are what keep me where I am at. This is the "letting go" principle I am talking about. If we do not let go of these sins we are committing and give them to God, we will continue to bang our heads against the wall…. over and over. Though Paul talks about what a wretched person he is, he then goes on to praise God that we have his Holy Spirit to override that sinful nature that is within us. If we allow the Holy Spirit to take control, our sinful nature slowly begins to loosen the grip it has on us.

This does not mean that we will not make another mistake again. But hopefully those mistakes will become less and less. I don't know about you, but I need this. Sometimes I go around the same mountain so many times - I get annoyed with myself. We all have to reach the end of our rope so that God can take hold of us and bring us to the other side of our struggle.

As a single person, I think we are more vulnerable to the temptations of sexual sin. We know it is wrong, but so many of us fall into the pitfalls of our hormones taking the lead in our lives. It is a dangerous place to be, and if we are not careful, it can have a monumental effect on us.

But on the same token, I do understand how hard it is to stay pure not only in this day and age, but also as a single person. It becomes more difficult when those around you are starting to tie the knot, and you are still waiting for the love of your life to show up. And to be honest, I am so sick of reading and hearing about those couples who were able to stay pure up until their wedding day, not ever flirting with those lines and boundaries we definitely should not be crossing.

In the Christian world it's like some of these people are some kind of saints who don't seem to have as hard of a time as I do when it comes to sexual activity (whatever that even means today). When you break out of the Christian bubble you realize how "good" of a person you are in that area, and you can easily get into the mentality of validating your sin because "hooking up" to you is not the same as a nonbeliever.

Right now I work in a restaurant, and you hear a lot of inappropriate talk amongst coworkers. The other day I was asked by a male coworker, "How many dates until you will have sex with a guy?" I responded by saying "never", but I don't think he realized how serious I was. While my other female coworker responded, "Two." Two! Really, I was a little in shock. But for most people, that is the norm these days. When witnessing conversations such as these I find myself feeling a lot better about my sin. I am just being honest, and don't think you have never compared yourself like that. But regardless, it is wrong for me to have that kind of thought process and mentality. Because the difference between my non-believing coworkers and me is just that, I believe in God and His commandments and word, and they do not. I have different convictions than they do, so I am to live accordingly whether or not I am "better" or more "good" than they are.

It is a tough life living as a Christian. Sometimes I think how much easier it would be if I wasn't. But then I wouldn't get to know all that I know. I wouldn't have the purpose that I have. I wouldn't understand life the way that I do. I would just move from one thing to the next hoping it would make me feel better than I did the day before. What a sad life that must be. Not to say living as a Christian doesn't make you sad, because I have sad days all the time. But I live knowing there is purpose attached to it and there is hope at the end of the day.

Learning to Let Go

There is freedom in letting go. I think the sooner we learn to let go and realize that we actually have no control over meeting "the one," the sooner we can start to enjoy life. I put so much pressure on myself to figure out my life. I think as women we have this desire to plan our lives and dream of the future, and we think we can't do that until we know *who* we will marry. Because let's face it, there are so many things that will change when we do get married. We have to plan around another person, and since we are problem solvers by nature, we want to foresee the future to prevent any wrong turns along the way. We can easily depend on a man to dictate our future and what our lives will look like because we are the ones who have babies and the ones whose careers will have to be put on hold when the time comes to start popping out some kids.

But as I am fast approaching my twenty-sixth birthday, still single as I have been for my whole life, I am learning to take a stand and stop wishing for what I don't have and start loving what I do have. For instance, my friends who are married or have kids could never move to Australia for a couple years like I did. At times I feel sorry for myself, and then I have to slap myself and remember that I am actually very lucky and blessed to be able to do this. Not many people get the opportunity to move to another country and experience a different culture, meet new people, and have an adventure of a lifetime. I don't think I will every say, "Man I really regret moving to Australia those many years ago." In the grand scheme of life, a couple years will be nothing, especially once I am in my next season of life where I am up to my elbows in diapers and spit up. I think I will look back and daydream of these days. What in your life right now is worth reminiscing about?

As a single woman, we have so many advantages! We still have the rest of our lives to have the stereotypical life we all so desperately want when we don't have it, and then when we have it, we dream of adventures and less responsibility. What is wrong with us? It's the grass is greener principle. We always want what we can't have and things are always better in someone else's lawn. It's just being human.

Once we see stop looking for greener pastures, we can start living how we were meant to live. It is definitely a journey to change old ways of thinking, but let's be women up for the challenge. I am not going to worry and try to figure out who God has for me to marry. I am not going to worry about what job I will have in the future. I won't get down on myself for being back in college (bible college) and working a random part time job that I don't like very much. It is all irrelevant in the grand scheme of life because I know that God has something way better in store for my future and something better for my present as well. He has things for me to see, be a part of, and do right now in this time of my life. And if I don't start looking for them, then I am going to miss them completely.

It's the little things in life that have the biggest impact. I feel the most at peace when I notice the small things God is trying to show me such as His beauty, whether it is a flower or hummingbird or a little baby laughing. God knows our hearts, and He wants to romance us if we let Him. For me, He will play an old song at one of my favorite cafes, and it warms my soul, or He displays a beautiful sunset on a stressful day when nothing seems to be going right. I started to learn this way of life by reading *One Thousand Gifts* and it's changed my outlook. That is what I love about God, He lets us choose how our life goes. But it is in the choosing that we get frustrated and upset because it really is on us whether we love our life or not.

When I am not loving my life, it's because I am looking at everything I don't have. Then I start focusing on all the wrong things. I really believe the key to life, especially living out singlehood well, is to appreciate what we do have and look for those beautiful moments God is trying to show us. Once we can do that on our own, not in a relationship, it will make it so much better when we are in a relationship. People who are in unhealthy relationships are most likely the ones who didn't appreciate what they had before a significant other; and they put too much pressure on the person they are with to make those things happen for them. But it isn't up to someone else to make us happy; that is when codependent and destructive relationships are bred. The more we can learn now while on our own, the better our future relationship with our husband will be. And that is not to say things won't still come up, but it will give the relationship a firmer foundation.

Dealing with Your Past

Sometimes before we let go of our past, we need to deal with it. Dealing with it is not easy; it can be painful and even heartbreaking all over again. But it is necessary if you want to be in a healthy relationship as a whole person. God will only reveal things that need to be dealt with if you are willing and if you are ready. If you don't ask, He won't show you. The choice is yours on whether you want to dig up this junk or keep hiding it in that treasure chest of yours.

The skeletons in our closets can be from past relationships, childhood, traumatic experiences, or sometimes even our own mistakes. But whatever your skeletons look like, none of them are too scary for God to face with you. It may be scary for you at first, but the Holy Spirit is there to comfort and guide you through this unknown territory. It must be conquered before you can have full access to freedom and the life He has for you.

It is much easier to just let things go without dealing with them first. It is much easier to forget they even happened. I would prefer to just keep looking forward and focusing on the person I am now rather than what I did in my past. But then God reminds me of areas that I still have not fully surrendered to Him. He wants to be Lord over our lives, and this means every part, and every area within them. He doesn't want just part of our heart, He wants all of it. For some of us, that is scary. We are afraid to look inside and see what is deep down there. But for all of us, it is imperative that we do it, and the sooner the better.

Unfortunately, all too often people keep pushing these hidden things further and further out of their consciousness and they come rearing their ugly heads, and a lot of times once they are already in a relationship. By then, it makes it that much harder to sort through. It will sting initially when you decide to take the plunge, but it is so much better to rip off that band-aid in one go rather than slowly peeling it off years later once it has become part of your skin.

Now you are probably wondering *how do we deal with these so-called skeletons that are lurking around?* I am still in the process myself, but what I do know is that we first must acknowledge them. Without acknowledging them and giving them a name, they still have power in the innermost parts of our being. You can't gain freedom from something if you don't know what you need freedom from. If you don't know what it is or how to name it, pray that God reveals it to you, and at the right time He will show you. It is a process so have patience with yourself and know that it will be revealed to you in God's timing.

Once you are able to name it, then comes the hard part: accepting responsibility and recognizing what wasn't your fault. Too often we take on things that weren't actually our fault, and we hold onto them and blame ourselves. Or we can do the opposite and blame everyone else, never taking any responsibility. Depending on which case you are, it is vital that you take this step in order to live a free and full life.

Recently God has brought up some heavy things from my past that I didn't realize were having an effect on me. In my early days of drinking and partying, towards the end of high school and beginning of college, I found myself blacking out often (meaning I wasn't coherent enough to know what I was doing and could not remember the next day). It got to the point that it was almost every time I drank. Because I was blacked out, there were many times I would get myself into situations that compromised my beliefs. I wouldn't remember how it started, but I would always have flashes of memories of what took place. These memories would show me that I had sex with guys whom I didn't even care about or hardly knew. And before my party days, I wanted to save sex for marriage. I knew what was right for me, but I did it anyway. Various reasons led me to this type of lifestyle: insecurity, low self-esteem and self-worth, amongst other things that all stemmed from my dysfunctional upbringing.

What I am realizing at this stage of my life, and after not having sex for over seven years, is that I've still been blaming myself. I know many of the times I had sex, I was raped due to my level of intoxication and lack of awareness and consciousness. Unfortunately this happens so often in our culture of binge drinking, especially with teens and college students, we oftentimes do not classify it as rape when in fact it is.

At that time in my life, I did not value myself and would allow guys to do what they wanted with me. But first I would practically 'roofie' myself. The day after, I would sometimes feel ashamed and sometimes feel nothing at all other than complete numbness. Like I said, so much of this was happening due to things from my childhood and the issues I had. It makes me sad to think of the girl who used to be treated this way. I feel so far removed from her at this point. I did have similar behaviors throughout the last 7 years. I may not have had sexual intercourse, but I did other sexual acts that I have regretted - old habits die hard. We all have our weaknesses, and this is mine - drinking and men. Mostly the combination of the two, one without the other is not a problem for me. When combined, I would consider that my kryptonite.

The last two years though, were healing years for me, filled with God really showing me how much He loves me. Once we really understand the love God has for us it changes the way we behave. We no longer look for love in the wrong places and things. We no longer feel empty and so alone. Love is always the answer, and when we decide to really live our lives for God and to honor Him, He will help us do it. He was so gentle and graceful when taking me on this journey of letting Him love me. It was so hard because everything I had experienced, whether it was of my own doing or not; but to Him it doesn't matter because He sees us blameless. God always knows our hearts and where they are at, and why we are the way we are. He doesn't hold us to those things either, but God knows where we are going at all times. The more we are able to accept the love He has for us, the more our past becomes our testimony rather than the thing we want to hide and run away from.

Forgiveness

Forgiveness is imperative always. In order for us to heal, we need forgiveness to do so. Forgiveness is one of the hardest things you can possibly give. It can feel like your flesh is actually ripping apart. It is painful, tearful, and refreshing all at the same time. Often when people have not gone through the forgiveness process, they are holding on to things that only infect them and no one else. It can cause bitterness to seep in and infect the heart and suffocate the life and love that was once there.

Not dealing with past hurts through forgiveness creates a roadblock where you can go forward no more. If you have ever heard someone say they feel stuck in life or maybe you have said it, it is usually because they have not forgiven someone and they are holding on to that situation to the extent that it has become a part of them. It is like they are walking around with a limp that they don't even realize they have. Everyone else can see it but them.

Maybe you do not need to forgive anyone, but maybe you need to forgive yourself. Forgiving yourself is often much harder than forgiving someone else. We are our own biggest critics at the end of the day, and so we have a harder time giving ourselves grace than anyone else. But do yourself a favor and forgive. You might be thinking *how do I even do that?* It is easy to say the words, "I forgive you," but to actually mean them is much harder.

First of all, it takes time to forgive someone or yourself. It takes time to process why you need to forgive them, what they did to you, how they hurt you, and so on. Those questions can be difficult to answer. You have to be honest with yourself and the other person. They may not even have a clue that they hurt you so badly enough to where you need to forgive them. Forgiveness takes a lot of effort, hard work, and strength, but you have it in yourself to do it. All you need is to be committed to it, and God will help you with the rest. You have to want to forgive and move forward, and usually that does not come until you have absolutely had enough of the poison that has been making you sick. Until you are ready to make a change, you will continue to go over and over the same issues masked in different forms your whole life.

Let your future relationship and family be motivation for you to learn forgiveness. Sometimes we find it hard to do things for our own benefit. At least, I used to because I was still on my journey of self-worth and value. I knew that one day I would have a family that I wanted to be as healthy as possible for. I grew up in unhealthiness, so I want my children to have a different life in that respect. At the beginning of working through my past hurts, my future husband and children were my motivation. You might be like me and need to do the same at first. I can now say that I do not make these changes for my future family, but I now also do it, first and foremost, for my relationship with God. I am much happier now, but I had to walk through a lot of years of struggle and ups and downs to get to this place with God where it is just He and I on the journey. But forgiveness was the key that started my journey, and it can be yours too.

5.

The Past Is Not Your Future

Have you ever had a conversation with a stranger that changed your life? I believe God puts certain people in our paths just so we can have a conversation that can stir us. Conversations that awaken desires in our hearts that we either forgot about or diminished. I had a conversation with a gentleman, (and I call him that not because he is older, but because he actually was a gentleman). He is only three years older than me but seems much older than the guys I know because of the way he talks and carries himself.

It was so refreshing talking with him because he actually talked about God and praying, and you could tell he loves Jesus more than anything. I couldn't believe it! I have been around the same church guys for three years now, and not once have I had a conversation like that with any of them. I felt this longing in me arise, not a painful one but an excited one. I remembered my dream of marrying someone who loves Jesus and actually wants to be like Him. A man of God who isn't afraid to admit he NEEDS God to help him in his life; man of God who knows where he is headed, even if he doesn't know how to get there. This future husband of mine is intelligent, funny, charming in a sincere way, and loyal.

He will pursue me, treat me like a princess, love me unconditionally, and know when he is wrong. He isn't perfect, but he works hard at growing with God. He leads and is confident. These are the desires of my heart when it comes to my future husband. And I know they weren't placed in my heart for nothing. God will fulfill these dreams and desires because He said He would. And He will do the same for you! But we can also get in His way if we are not careful. We could settle for less. We could date whomever because they are paying attention to us. We could let a guy use us if he wants. We could easily forget what God promised and do our own thing. I have done that many times. Accepted less than the best because I got weary and stopped believing and waiting expectantly for this man to appear. I still struggle with it.

It is hard to hold onto something you can't see or have never experienced. It is our human nature to go off of our past experiences where we form these beliefs about life and love. When we have not had good experiences in the area of love, it clouds our perspective and can taint these hopes and dreams we once had if we are not aware of it. But thank God we have a loving God of restoration. He can renew our minds and hearts if we allow him. We have to be willing to let the truth be unveiled in our lives. Sometimes it is unpleasant and can be discouraging. If that is the case, invite God to heal those places in your heart that have been deadened and lied to. Those past experiences do not have to dictate your future. God has much bigger plans than what has already taken place. You may have to go through some valleys and dark places to get to the top of your mountain, but you can do it through Christ who strengthens you and gives you this vision to see where you are headed.

Personally I still am dealing with my past experiences and even current experiences. But God has reminded me what I am meant for. He has resurrected those things that He has placed in my heart. It has refreshed me and given me fuel to keep on going. He has been showing me some painful things as well, in order for me to release them, give them to Him to diminish and renew within my spirit.

For instance, last night He revealed to me that I have a spirit of codependence. He showed me that I want to be needed so badly that I put someone else's needs before my own. I compromise beliefs and myself in order to make someone else happy even if it leaves me hurting. If I am hurting, I then deny how I feel and become numb to my behavior. I can become obsessed with what the other person in my codependent relationship is doing or not doing.

It makes sense that I would be this way because I grew up with an alcoholic father and codependent mother. I learned what a relationship looks like from them even if I knew it wasn't right and it was unhealthy. As hard as we try to not become like our parents, it is easy to fall into such behavior because we were conditioned for it and never knew any different.

But the good news is that God can change the very thing we were conditioned to be and make us into a new creation. He reveals these strongholds and issues we face, in order to change them and help us not struggle with them any longer. When He revealed the codependent spirit within me, it wasn't in a judging way whatsoever. It was in a loving way that gently spoke to me within my heart and told me to repent and renounce the codependent spirit and put on a spirit dependence on Him. So that is what I did, I gave it to God and laid it at His feet so that I may be freed from codependent relationships from this point on. Where I can be in a healthy relationship: where I can openly communicate my feelings and thoughts and be heard and respected, where I won't worry about what the other person is doing or not doing, where I won't be manipulated into doing things I do not agree with, and where I won't be in pain but will have pure joy.

I confess this to you openly and honestly so that you won't be afraid to ask God what you need to change and need help with. Maybe there is a relationship in your life similar to mine, and it is not your fault that you struggle with this type of behavior. But it is your responsibility to take charge of it and give it over to God so that He can heal you and bring you to where you need to be. He has called us to happiness not pain and anger. That does not mean we will never experience those things, but if we do, it is only to teach us and grow us. He is not mad at us when those things happen; it is for our own benefit so that we can grow into our fullness.

Don't Let Yourself Go, but Let Yourself Grow

In the meantime of waiting for your love story to unfold, it is so important to grow! It is easy to get discouraged in the process and not make personal growth a priority. We all have the temptation to ignore how our present lives now are possibly affecting our lives in the future with our loved ones. But if we could dedicate ourselves to growing while we wait, then it would make our future with our husband that much better.

Growth in the areas where we struggle with and growth in the areas we are weaker is what will prepare us for what is ahead. If we can work out some things in the dry desert season that singleness can be, we are already ahead of the game when our promise land of a husband appears before us. And the more we grow now, the better kind of man we will attract. There is no point in wasting any time in these single days. Our days as a single woman are very limited, whether you believe it or not. I know that society's norms trip us up by telling us we should have been married a year ago, but when we look at the span of our whole lives, we really have very limited days of being single. So as cliché as it sounds, we really do need to cherish each one and live it out to its fullest potential.

Let yourself grow. Read books, journal, go out in nature and appreciate its beauty, explore, and go on an adventure. I have felt the most confident, excited and wondrous when I have gone out on my own without any particular destination, but I have let the Holy Spirit just guide me and walk with me. He has shown me things that make my heart sing. It is those little things that we love that keep us going. When we are so focused on all the things that we don't have, we can get into a downward spiral that starts spinning so fast we are at the bottom before we even know we are spinning.

Everyone has stuff to deal with, whether you come from a happy family or not. Every family is dysfunctional to some degree, and this puts marks on us that sometimes need to be healed and worked through or even just acknowledged. There is power in seeing truths about ourselves that may not be the prettiest or most pleasant. But until those marks see the light of day, they cannot be healed; but they will only be covered up by the shadows they hide in. They will come out eventually though, and it is better they emerge now while you are single then later down the road when you are in a relationship, and it's that much harder to cope with.

If you have marks or scars that are too big for you to handle on your own, I do suggest counseling. I know I would not have survived or become as healthy as I am today if I had not gone to counseling on and off for the last few years with a commitment to changing. And I would go again, and I'm sure I will go again in the future. It helped me deal with things I didn't even know I had in me. When you come from a highly dysfunctional family, like I had, counseling is necessary for sanity and overall well-being. I know counseling can be unpopular and even shameful depending on your understanding of it. But today it has become more and more acceptable, much more than the generations past.

All of this to say, don't have the mindset that it takes any sort of perfection in this area in order to find someone. People can still meet their spouse in the midst of their own personal turmoil or before they are really committed to growing. But I do find it is much harder on their relationship when they haven't committed to that journey yet. It is just wise and very helpful to grow while in this season, regardless of whether it will get you out of the single season any sooner. It may or may not, but that is up to God and what He has planned for you. It will, however, make you much happier in the long run and jump start your own life to head in the right direction for what God is calling you to. He calls us all to live happy and healthy lives dedicated to growing and stretching so we can walk into all He has before us.

6.

Relationship with God

Our relationship with God is what dictates our life and future. Our past and where we come from is irrelevant when we seek God and put Him first. We will still make mistakes, even some that we thought were now in our past. But if we keep God at the forefront, and always come back to Him and not hide from Him, everything eventually falls into place until the next upward battle happens, and we must press on until we reach the top again.

My favorite verse is Psalm 37:4:

"Delight yourself in the Lord and He will give you the desires of your heart."

Delight means to get pleasure, satisfaction, and enjoyment from the Lord. Please Him highly. This means to not look to a relationship with a person or not look to things, accomplishments, money, or anything else to give you your pleasure and wholeness. It is a very dangerous place to be when those things control our lives. Because those things can fade away, and then what will you be left with? When we can't answer that question with our relationship with God, then we are in trouble. We must lean on and rely on Him to fill us. Fill us with His presence, peace, and wholeness. Until we are whole, we are not able to have healthy relationships.

Our relationship with God is a journey. It takes time, trust, and tenacity. It does not happen overnight, just like any relationship, things must be built from the ground up. Foundation is everything, so until we can get the small things down, we aren't able to move forward into bigger things. God wants all of us, every part and every place in our heart. He is jealous for you. He does not want anyone else having my heart before He does because we are His creation and His people. So He doesn't want us to worship anyone or anything else because we are meant to worship Him. That is why He is so pained when we give our heart to men or guys who do not deserve it. This isn't to say we will never give our heart to a man because we will need to give it to our husband. But God must have it first.

God needs to have our heart first to build it into what it needs to be in preparation for marriage. This could look like rebuilding it, fixing and mending some old wounds that once shattered us, or reviving it from its mundane and emotionless protection that has become a hard-to-break habit. God knows what He is doing and how to do it. But that is where trust comes in and is a foundational building block. Trust is a scary thing because you don't know what is on the other side. I think we are actually more afraid to be healed and whole because that is when God really catapults our lives. Many times we would rather hide and stay in our safe, comfortable bubble of self-doubt and fear. You can stay there and have a relationship with God, but it will be limited. God is limitless and craves to give us a life that is unexpected, full of surprises, and rich in His goodness. It is the unknown that scares us though. But without the unknown, life would not be as sweet. Knowing God more breeds more uncertainties in life because that is the way in which He works. But it is so beautiful when you can let Him in and trust Him because that is when He breaths miracles into your life that you never thought would be possible.

God is LOVE

I have had much trouble with this concept in my life. God is love. Probably because the world views love as something completely different than what it actually is. In the world, we watch movies about people who fall in love, and it is always so dramatic and emotional. So many highs and lows that dictate how life is going based on the roller coaster some of these relationships can put us on. Not only does the world adopt this form of love, but so do our families, friends, or parents, and it confuses us as young children on what love actually is.

In my own experience, growing up there was always so much chaos attached to this so-called love my parents were enveloped in. There was always fighting, yelling, and then grand gestures to reconcile the arguments that were had the night before. Apologies came in cards, letters, and flowers. Sometimes not only did my dad bring those things for my mom, but my sister and I as well, since most of the time we were just as involved in the blow up as my mother was. This story is just one of the many examples of how our beliefs and ideas of love have become null and void when compared to its actual meaning and definition that God is LOVE. When we have that belief in place, love becomes very different to us. It is not as dramatic and upsetting as one may think. Unfortunately, most of us find the stability quite boring at first because unhealthy can be unpredictable which can come across as exciting and passionate. But as we grow and learn what love really is, the more "boring" we ultimately want.

For me personally, I still struggle with this. I don't think I will know what to do when someone whom I actually love, loves me back and not only through words, but with actions. Love is not a noun; it is a verb, an action expressed through doing not just saying. Love is expressed by acts of kindness and thoughtfulness. It is not only a word, but I was once told, it is a decision. You love someone, and you decide to pursue him or her, commit to him or her, and stay with them. How boring!…Or so I thought.

But for some reason the idea of such a secure, stable state makes some of us so afraid because we have never experienced anything like it. Not with another human at least. My experience with God has taught me otherwise. But the world and those around greatly affect this principle that *God is love.* Unfortunately our past experiences can cause us to believe things that are just not true. We may say we know that God loves us, but do we really believe it through the way we act and speak? I know I personally have trouble with that, and I know until I make the decision that my past experience does not have to dictate my future, God will continue to wait patiently for me to grab onto the promises He has for me in regards to love and everything else for that matter.

God doesn't want us to accept counterfeit love through shallow relationships with the opposite sex. He wants us to have a beautiful love story unfold that is better than the ones we see in the movies. He wants us to hold onto the promises He has made to us. And if you do not think He has made any promises to you yet, pray and ask Him for some. You will be surprised by what has been in your heart all along. He wants you to be happy. He does not want you to be alone, but first you have to accept and let go of some things.

We discover what love really is in 1 Corinthians 13:7 (MSG):
Love never gives up.
Love cares more for others than for self.
Love doesn't want what it doesn't have.
Love doesn't strut,
Doesn't have a swelled head,
Doesn't force itself on others,
Isn't always "me first,"
Doesn't fly off the handle,

Doesn't keep score of the sins of others,
Doesn't revel when others grovel,
Takes pleasure in the flowering of truth,
Puts up with anything,
Trusts God always,
Always looks for the best,
Never looks back,
But keeps going to the end.

When I read this, I realize I still have a lot of growing to do in the love department. I think we can agree that most of us do. But when we can see that God is love, how beautiful it is to know that He loves us. He loves us despite our love towards Him. He loves us unconditionally and endlessly. He loved us first.

As humans we fall, and we don't get it right all the time, but God does. We can see the example of love worked out through Jesus' life and all throughout the Bible. He never betrays or abandons. He never rejects or declines; yet He always invites and welcomes us with open arms. As we continue on this love journey, we will learn just how much He actually loves us and how much He has done for us out of this love.

7.

Knowing Holy Spirit

Growing up somewhat in church and as a Christian, I had very little interaction with and knowledge of the Holy Spirit. Looking back, I definitely felt His presence at times and can see His involvement in my life. But it has only really been the last 5 years that I have gone on this journey of getting to know Him personally rather than just a "the." It is so common for us to call him THE Holy Spirit; in fact, I still do most of the time, out of habit. But I am building my relationship with Him and trying to see Him in a different way.

Now you may be wondering why I am writing about Him in this book on being single, but I have found that He is a key part to our story when it comes to finding love. Let me explain! A few years ago I was at a youth camp as a youth leader. At the time I was leading young girls and trying to teach them their value when I didn't fully understand my own value. At this time I was involved with a guy who did not value me for the woman I was, but he mostly was interested in my body and what I could do for him. I had not had this type of relationship (or lack of relationship, considering there really was no commitment) in years because I had started going to church and thought I had been freed from many of the strongholds I once had involving attention from the opposite sex. One of the nights during the camp, we had extended worship and during it one of the women on church staff came up to me and felt that the Holy Spirit was telling her that He wants to have intimacy with me. I can't remember what else she had said, but I started bawling like a baby while somewhat trying to conceal my reaction because I didn't want other people to see that there was obviously something wrong with me. I had been hiding, not only from people, but from the one person who could actually help free me. Holy Spirit knew everything that had taken place in my life - from the first time I had my heart broken which was by my own father, up until then when I was letting someone else treat me less than I deserved.

At that moment, when the word intimacy was spoken to me, I felt so lost yet found. I didn't know exactly what He meant because intimacy to me meant taking off my clothes and letting a guy take what he wanted from me, leaving me feeling empty and worthless. I went through a few years of this behavior where I so desperately wanted to be loved, but I didn't know how to let anyone in. The only form of intimacy I knew was what the world had shown me. But when Holy Spirit uttered the word intimacy, I knew He was after a different kind.

I then grew frustrated because I didn't know how or what to do. I didn't know what He wanted from me. I felt like I had nothing left to give him because I was in such turmoil internally and felt so empty. Years of damage to my soul had taken place, and I didn't know how to repair it. But still, I knew He would know what to do. So little by little, I wrestled with Him on this idea and failed many a time. I definitely got worse before I got better. It took me about another year of being disrespected and mistreated before God fully removed me out of the situation to be rebuilt and healed.

Still on this continuing journey of intimacy, I find myself more whole than ever before. I understand my value, and I haven't let a man abuse me or objectify me like that since. But I am well aware that I could easily fall into that trap again if I am not constantly pursuing Holy Spirit. And not only pursuing Him, but for me to also let Him pursue me - more importantly.

If you too struggle with this idea of intimacy, don't get discouraged when you feel yourself pull away. Holy Spirit isn't afraid of your fears or your inabilities to love Him the way He wants you to. But He will actually find you where you are at, whether you are hiding or running away, and gently bring you back to Him through his pursuit of your heart. He wants nothing more than your heart. You can make every possible mistake there is, and He will always be waiting for you to let Him redeem your life to its full potential - its fullness of beauty and intrigue that you possess.

You may even find yourself thinking *I have given Him all of me*, and He will gently show you there is still more of your heart you are reluctantly holding onto. But if you are committed to Him, He will do what He needs to in order to bring about completion and wholeness. Our hearts are like an onion with many different layers that are yet to be pulled away to unravel all that is within you. There is more to you than you even realize, and He knows the intricacies that make up the person who you are. It sounds a bit terrifying when you are on a journey of letting Him in, but as soon as you surrender, you will see what I mean. He is so gracious and kind and does not want us to be in pain, but sometimes it is painful to allow Him into all the different parts of yourself: the good, the bad, and the ugly. He is in it all and does not mind it either. He created you and knows your weaknesses and strengths. The enemy also knows them, so it is our responsibility to be aware of what might be calling our attention, is it from God or the enemy? On your intimacy journey, you are able to learn the distinction between the two, and it will help you unlock your potential easier because you know what to look out for when the enemy comes to take you out. Intimacy with the Holy Spirit is what will carry you through and bring you on the other side and on top of any mountains you may be climbing.

Let Him Romance You

Holy Spirit wants to romance you. I don't know about you, but when I first heard this concept, I thought it was a bit strange. How can a spirit romance you? Honestly, I was a bit afraid. I had never really been romanced before, at least not in the way I would want to be. But the best part about Holy Spirit is He knows us so well. He knows everything about us - from our greatest fear to what makes our hearts sing.

I love this verse in Song of Songs 2:10-13:

"My lover said to me, 'Rise up, my darling! Come away with me, my fair one! Look, the winter is past, and the rains are over and gone. The flowers are springing up, the season of singing birds has come, and the cooing of turtledoves fills the air. The fig trees are forming young fruit, and the fragrant grapevines are blossoming. Rise up, my darling! Come away with me, my fair one!'"

We may not see those things every day, but that is the kind of relationship Holy Spirit wants with us. He wants us to come away with Him, and He will show us such beauty we have never known before. He wants to melt our hearts with the things that we love. For me, I am such a girl in the sense that I love flowers, candles, and chocolate. I love home decor and old antique shops. So I love when Holy Spirit leads me into a shop with beautiful furniture and decorations. He cares about the little things as well as the big. When we are feeling alone, He is just waiting for us to look up, "Rise up," and see that we aren't alone and that He is right there with us.

I truly believe that in our days of singleness, if we allow Holy Spirit to romance us, it will only make our relationship with our future husband and our marriage to be that much better. He is setting the bar for us. Obviously we will never find a man as good as Holy Spirit because no one is perfect, but if we want to find one that resembles Him, then we are going to need to know Holy Spirit. The more we know Him, the easier it will be to spot red flags in a guy so we don't waste our time and energy.

He is beckoning us to come on an adventure with Him. He is waiting for us to allow Him to lead us to secret gardens and unknown territories - start with the little things. Just the other day I decided to go for a walk; I wanted to go somewhere I had never been before. I wanted to go on a hike, but everything was too far away, so I asked the Holy Spirit to lead me. And when I did, I came across the most beautiful pond with a long red bridge going across it. I saw ducks, fish, and even a black swan. It was so majestic and beautiful. Even though I was in the city, and there were still people around where I was walking, I felt like it was just the two of us taking in the beauty of God's creation and appreciating the fresh air. The week leading up to this, I felt so frustrated with my life and what I was doing because I wasn't looking up and around. I was looking from the confinement of my bedroom and only seeing as far as my mirror, which was showing me someone who wasn't content in life even though I knew I should be and wanted to be.

It is so easy to lose sight of what it is God is actually trying to speak to us through His spirit. Sometimes we have to get out of our "comfort zone" which for me was my bedroom and get outside and go for a wander with the Holy Spirit. When you create that space for Him in your life, whatever it looks like for you, He is then able to speak to you and show you things you have never seen or even knew were there before. He wants to take you on a never-ending adventure that only gets better and better. But it is also filled with risk after risk. You will have to be brave which sometimes isn't easy. But just wait for Him to sweep you off your feet into wide-open spaces in your life that you never even knew existed.

Live Married

Recently I had the thought of - *why not live as if I am already married?* I know that sounds strange because I am not married. But when I think about my relationship with God and my daily companionship with the Holy Spirit, I definitely am married in some respect. I may not tell others openly that I am "married" to Jesus or wear a ring because I would probably sound crazy, but why should I have to continue to long for something I can have and already have access to. I know it is not the same thing as having a physical man I'm married to, but while I wait for my earthly husband, I can practice and learn through my marriage to My Savior.

I am constantly hoping and wishing for the day when someone can love me the way I want to be loved, yet God has been there all along just waiting for me to love Him back. He knows I love Him, but now I need and want to show Him I love Him. I think all He wants from us is just to stop and smell the roses. Stop worrying about the mundane things that this life and world have to offer us, but choose to live through heavenly eyes and see the beauty He so desperately is trying to show us in our day to day.

If I am able to choose to live as if I am married to the One who knows me better than anyone else, why wouldn't I? And when the time comes for my earthly *Prince Charming* to step into the picture, I will already know what marriage is supposed to look like, and it will be an easier transition. Not only that, but I won't have to wrestle with where marriage should be placed in my life because my relationship with God will be secure and unshakeable and He will be my *first love*.

I have found that I, in the past and still am tempted to today, idolize the idea of marriage and relationships. I have thought that marriage will be the answer to my happiness and success in life; that if only once I had a boyfriend, future husband, will my life look the way I want it to. But none of that is true. The world may view relationships as the end all be all, but Heavenly speaking it means nothing. And I think that has been my problem with some of the years I have been waiting. I have put the idea and love of marriage above the one who created it. I have "worshiped" marriage and love for another human being. I think God has been trying to get my attention all this time and show me that He needs and wants that place in my life before He can let anyone else take space in my heart.

I do not think this is for everyone, but for some reason this is how God handles me. God wants us to tell Him everything and come to Him when we need help. He wants us to embrace Him as He embraces us. He wants us to trust Him wholeheartedly, and He wants to love us unconditionally. God wants to romance us and take us on this beautiful journey filled with joy and love. But we are too busy looking around and being distracted from anything good for us.

Personally I have been through a long winter season, and I have been waiting for God to do something amazing in my life. I have been waiting for this spring season to take place where I am singing with joy. But it still hasn't come. And now I wonder if the Holy Spirit has just been waiting for me all of this time. Waiting for me to come join Him in the new season He has prepared for me. I can sit and wallow in my unhappiness about where I am at in life and the fact that it looks nothing like what I thought it would at the age of twenty-six. Or I can rise above the lies I have been listening to and enter into this beautiful, loving, exciting marriage relationship with the *Man of my dreams*. And as I walk with Him and become more in sync with Him, I will eventually be able to be with the man on earth He has chosen for me. It won't be so complicated when I actually meet this mystery man because the Holy Spirit will guide me, and I will be able to recognize His thoughts and what He says about him.

8.

A Man, Not to Be Confused by a Boy

Now here is the part where it is going to sound like I am bashing men. I promise you there will be a positive spin on this subject, but we do need to discuss some things. Unfortunately, they just don't make them like they used to. Generally speaking of course, men are progressively becoming lazier in their pursuit of a women. They are increasingly letting the girl chase them rather than the other way around, the way it was intended. It is not entirely their fault either. With increasing technology it is becoming easier for men and women to find each other through dating apps and websites. Men and women can just scroll through and see who they fancy based on physical appearance and swipe right.

The downside to this technology is that there are so many more options for men and women today. Because of the Internet they are able to see how many people really are out there, and it creates a "wandering eye" syndrome. Now this definitely goes both ways for both genders. It is such a shame that it has become increasingly confusing for people to commit to one another because they are tempted by what else might be out there.

The upside to these dating apps and websites is that you can get straight to the point. They like what they see, they are open about what they are looking for, and if it aligns, then boom! Magic. Sparks fly. I have seen it with some of my friends and heard beautiful stories come from it.

There are a lot of boys today, and the men supply is fleeting. I don't know if it is because we come from a more fatherless generation, higher divorce rate, or what, but men just don't know how to be men. Again not all men, but we all know the boys out there who are just looking for some fun and nothing serious; the boys who cannot commit to one girl because they have to play the field. The boys who play with hearts because they don't know how to take care of them. I am sure you have had experience with a boy or two like this. They say one thing and do another. They are confusing and frustrating. They are scared of the future but don't even know what they want or how to get it.

"Boys will be boys" is not only a cliché saying; but it is fact. So what do we do with these boys who keep playing with our heartstrings? The boys who could potentially be the perfect man for you if they just figured out a few things. Honestly, we move on from them. By all means you can still be friends, but a conversation needs to be had. Boundaries need to be put in place, and they need to be called out. It will be awkward at first and maybe even for a little while after, but ultimately you need to move on. Because even if those few things changed, who knows if he would pursue you or if those things would stick. And if he does pursue you, then amazing, but if he doesn't, you don't want to waste any time or energy on him.

As women we want a man to know where things in the relationship are going at all times and even if the man doesn't know how it will play out, he goes for it anyway. A man that takes risks and isn't afraid to fail. I mean, obviously, they are human beings, and they aren't perfect. There will be times in their lives when they aren't as secure as you would like them to be. But I am talking about the pursuit of a woman. They may be scared, but they go for it anyway because the risk of losing the girl of their dreams is more frightening than not.

A boy will pass off his insecurities and project them onto you. He will make you believe that you are the problem and not him. A boy will manipulate you to get what he wants and won't apologize for it. He will hold your hand and act like your boyfriend, but he won't give you the commitment and reassurance you need. He won't respect your boundaries because he doesn't have any of his own.

But a man will cherish you and adore you; he will want to protect you. He will be honest and open so that you never have to guess what he is thinking and feeling. He will set boundaries and uphold them. He will initiate conversations that lead to the direction of your relationship. He will take responsibility for his actions and will apologize first...most of the time. A man will always reassure you without you asking for it. A man will be a gentleman and will treat you like a princess.

These are just a few differences between a boy and a man. And I am sure you could add to the list just based off of personal experiences. With a boy, there is a fun time, but with a man, there is a lifetime of adventure. A man will be in it for the long haul and won't be afraid of a future with you.

Watch Out

I was always one of those girls who would get so worked up when hearing about a guy mistreating a girl, whether it was them cheating on them, using them, or lying to them. I never thought I would let a guy walk all over me or have control of a relationship. I was a little over-dramatic, until I met a boy who changed all that. I fell fast, and I fell hard. I don't know if it was love or what, but I let him call the shots even if it hurt me. I let him use me how he wanted, without completely giving up all my morals and values, only some. I let him repeatedly come back to me; even after he would flirt and try make a move on other girls in front of me.

I am one of those optimistic romantics who believe love can conquer all. But unfortunately, that can only happen when both people are on board. I struggled with thinking of him as the not-so-good person that he was. I saw him as the potential he had rather than the reality he was. But there comes a point when enough is enough! God has not called me to see potential in someone, so much so, that it would actually hurt my own potential and well-being. He did not ask me to stick around in something unhealthy with a boy who was not capable of being the man of God that I needed him to be. I do believe, one day he will be an amazing man of God, but at the same time I do not need to stick around and wait for that to happen. But why do I continue to hang on to something that isn't even there? Because this boy is a player, and doing what he does, he played me. Every time I would try to talk about our weird relationship, he feed me a bunch of BS that I wanted to hear. So therefore, it kept me around, holding onto that little glimmer of hope he ever so slightly had dangled in front of me, so that I didn't go too far in order for him to weasel his way back into my life and heart again. This way he gets what he wants, some messing around and convenience, while I get my fill of feeling wanted and needed which all girls crave so deeply. In the hands of the wrong guy, it can be catastrophic to a lonely girl's life.

So here I was, looking like an idiot while he goes on with his life not even realizing the damage he had done. And then when these players are confronted about their behavior, they play dumb. And if they aren't getting what they want from you, they will go somewhere else and get it. Then if you are really lucky, (saying this in a sarcastic tone) he will come back to you once you are slowly becoming less angry, and he will turn on his charm and try once again. The playee is then in a rock and a hard place, trying to decide how to act around this so-called player. Do you ignore them and act mad? Or do you act like nothing happened and tell yourself it won't happen again? Or do you just flee the country? Joking, but not joking since I kind of did that!

Either way, no matter which approach you choose, you will face this over and over again whether it is he or a different player. God has this way of making us face our weaknesses over and over until we are strong enough to get it right and not keep making the same mistakes. As frustrating and difficult as it is, thank God He does that. Because otherwise we would be stuck in the same patterns and cycles of unhealthiness that will take us nowhere which is exactly what the devil wants. Honestly I used to judge girls who would let guys treat them the way this particular boy treated me. I made excuses because I didn't want to believe what everyone was telling me because if I did, then that would mean I was like every other girl I despised in my previous years. But this just goes to show we cannot judge others for where they are at in life and their struggles because you never know what you will encounter in the future, and you never know how much of a struggle that is for someone else. We all are on our own journey, and everyone has different strengths and weaknesses.

Looking Back

I am now twenty-seven, reading what I had written above. It seems so foreign and far removed from me, this situation I had with this boy-man. I call him that because it sounds like he really needed to grow up. The choice I made was to flee the country. Jokingly and seriously, I did have to flee the country. Initially it was not because of him, but I do see how God used the distance and time in Australia to break the chains I once was shackled by. This "relationship" was the longest, deepest, and most destructive I have ever had. Now that I am past it and have not entered into anything that remotely resembles this relationship, I am so thankful that I went through it and grew from it. I still do not like thinking about how I acted or the mistakes I made, but I do look back and learn from it.

I still at times feel a sense of betrayal because of how things played out. Shortly after I moved to Australia, he started dating one of my "friends." We still have mutual friends, and I hope I do not have to see either of them very often. But I also have to forgive them for the pain and betrayal they caused me. I think it has been hard to admit that they did hurt me because it shows weakness in me. But it is the truth, and the truth will set me free. I do not like seeing them because it does remind me of such a dark, hard time in my life. But it also reminds me of how thankful I am that it did not work out with him. He was totally wrong for me. We didn't bring the best out in each other. And though I held on way too long to how good the beginning of our relationship was, I eventually was able to let it go. It was extremely hard at times. I did not see God in the midst of it, helping me, but He really was there. He gave me the grace I needed to let go and be free.

I now wish my two old friends happiness. I have even prayed for their relationship, which I probably never thought I would be able to do in the past. But God restores our hearts and takes away pain when we give Him time and permission to. I now know to look out for the red flags I saw but I chose to ignore back then. Even if the only purpose of that relationship was to learn what not to do, it was worth it!

9.

Make Him Work For It

Men like a challenge. They are built to overcome and conquer. The world tells us that the easier you are to men, in terms of your sexuality or giving them what they want, the more chance you have of landing one. But do you really want to be with a guy who wants to be with a girl who just gives it up easily?

I don't know about you, but I want a real man; a man who won't give up easily. A man who goes after what he wants and doesn't get overtaken by his fears or insecurities. I want a man who doesn't get discouraged if I am not constantly affirming him. I think the way a man pursues a woman shows what he will be like later on in the relationship as well. If a man waits patiently and doesn't give up on you, even when you are unsure of your feelings towards him, that shows his willingness to be in it for the long haul and hopefully "till death do you part."

In today's society of instant gratification and things happening so quickly with technology, no one has to work much for anything. I think this has filtered into relationships, and more importantly, the lack of relationships happening. Both men and women are becoming more and more impatient causing them to settle in all areas of life, especially when it comes to dating.

It's tragic the way we carry on in life, going from one person to the next, waiting for the "next best thing" until we look around and we are the only single ones left. I am not saying we all do this, but generally speaking this sadly happens more often than it should. I have even asked myself lately if I am just looking for the next best or if I would be settling choosing one of the guys who have been interested in me as of late? But I always remind myself to go back to the promise God has given me. The man I will marry will be the one who pursues me the way I want to be pursued. He will fight for me. And when that happens, I will know in my heart that it is the right person and right time.

Now I say all of this, not so you play games of hard to get. There is a difference between not being an easy catch and playing hard to get. It is okay to make it known that you are interested, but you can do it in subtle ways. With the right person, it won't take much effort to make it known you are interested. He will know just by your interactions with him because you won't be able to contain the joy you feel around him. We complicate it so often by thinking we need to be more like this or that to get a guy's attention. But when it is the right person, it will happen organically without much effort. Guys do not want a girl who plays games or is super complicated in knowing what they want. A woman who knows what she wants, just like a man who does, is very attractive. So if he isn't what you want, the whole package, move on. No one is perfect, but you do not need to try to fit someone into the box you've created with your idea of the perfect guy. But with that said, never settle.

Never Settle

The struggle of not settling is very real. As we grow impatient, waiting for the dreams of our heart to come to pass, we are faced with the temptation to settle. Once we realize and understand what we want, what we want is hard to come by, so we slowly grow weary in waiting. When the next best thing comes around, and he has almost all of the qualities and characteristics (close but no cigar) we have been waiting for, we have a choice to make, *settle or keep waiting?*

I have found this to be the hardest part of all while waiting for the right guy to come around. I meet a guy who I think is great and attractive, but I know deep down he is not the right one for me. But it is nice to have his attention. This is when things get tricky. Because I know for me, I start to justify and make excuses, "Well you never know, he could be it." But really, I do know because God has placed specific things on my heart about the person I will spend the rest of my life with. I will know when I meet him if he is it or isn't. What is so frustrating is that I could date the "almost guy" and have fun, but then I know that ultimately it will end, and I will have wasted my time and his. So what is the point?

God uses everything for good. And I believe even the short-lasting encounters I have with these guys as I wait, is all teaching me something. It is teaching me to spot "red flags" quicker. It is teaching me to say *no* when I need to, to hold tight to my convictions and values. It is teaching me to be a stronger woman with good boundaries. It is teaching me what I want in a relationship and what I don't want. I am learning to trust God more while I wait, and He is teaching me patience that will be used in many other areas of life as I continue on this journey.

We are not meant to settle in any area of life. We are called to dream, and once we start dreaming, we must dream bigger and bigger. Dreaming is what brings things into being. But there is an art to dreaming. It cannot take up all your headspace all the time. It must be purposeful with the right motives. We can sometimes focus on dreams too much where it becomes obsession. We can dream of the man we will marry, but when we put a specific someone in that box and start dreaming of them before we know whether he is "it" or not, our thoughts can become dangerous. So when we dream, dream about the future with the unknown man God has for you and not the specific man you hope and wish he will be.

As we wait and we don't settle, God continues to set the scene for a beautiful love story to unfold that only He can write: one that will be full of unexpected and surprising moments that you could have never dreamed up yourself. It is all right there in your future just waiting for you. If it hasn't happened yet, then the story isn't full enough to be revealed. There are paragraphs and poems still to be written in this beautiful love story that you will experience and live out one day.

While you wait, let the ultimate love of your life, Jesus Christ, romance you and set the scene for an earthly man to sweep you off your feet. Let Jesus be your *first love* while He shows you what it really looks like to love and be loved. He will prepare you for a long lasting, forever marriage that will be rich in kindness and grace. If you cannot receive it from the source, then you will never be able to give love the way you are intended to. Marriage is give and take but without the expectation of receiving anything. When we go into any relationship expecting to receive rather than give - we are robbing ourselves and others of the greatness of unconditional, endless love that is meant to be.

Endless love has no bounds or restrictions. It is complete freedom to be who you are without insecurity or fear. It is the oasis we long for, feelings of safety and protection. Endless love is a wide-open space for mistakes and mystery. The good kind of mystery that makes us excited to be alive because we don't know what we will discover next.

A relationship that will transition into marriage can only reach its God-given full potential when the people in it can enter into this endless love affair with Jesus. Without the source pouring into us, we cannot love the way we are meant to. He gives us everything we need without hesitation. The only hesitation that may take place is from us. Many times we hesitate to take hold of the free gifts God wants to bestow onto us because of fears and past experiences that have caused us to question who we are and who God is. It is a dangerous place to be that can only be overcome with the act of surrendering and letting go of the things that are trying to hold us back. Easier said than done, but when we rise up and take a stand against such things we are FREE. Freedom is the most precious gift of all because when we are free, we can accept all the other incredible gifts God wants to give us.

Keep Your Standards High

Standards show us our core values. Values are what we build our life upon. If our standards are low when it comes to a potential husband, we will get what we aim for. Now if they are high, we will get that and even more than we imagined. Standards are important to set before dating someone. They are used as a compass that can direct you on whether to move forward or not. Boundaries keep you in line and focused on what it is you actually want in a spouse.

I have seen over the years, girls lower their standards out of desperation or impatience of wanting a relationship. Or they lower them because it is immediate gratification rather than long term. I have done this myself, and thank God He has not let me settle for less than what He has for me for the long run.

Another issue I want to raise is that of faith. Does the person you are dating believe in the same things you do? Does he have a relationship with God like you? In the Bible it talks about men being the spiritual leader.

1 Corinthians 11:3 (NLT) says, "But there is one thing I want you to know: The head of every man is Christ, the head of woman is man, and the head of Christ is God."

If he does not have a close walk with God, then it will be much harder for him to lead you. And it will be harder for you to have a healthy relationship. You can't lead someone who is not being led himself by God. It takes a humble man to let God lead him because to many it could look like weakness. But in truth, it is actually more telling of a man's strength when he allows himself to be vulnerable and ask for help from his Creator.

This idea of submission has many negative connotations due to women being oppressed in our society in the past and unfortunately still happens today. It has become much better in more recent generations, but the fear of women being overtaken by a man has changed the meaning behind submission in our current culture. But submission is a beautiful thing when in the right hands. When we are submitted to God, He is able to do things through us that we would not normally be able to accomplish on our own. And that goes the same for when we are submitted to our husband in the future. That is why it is so important for you to marry a man of God who is following Jesus while taking the lead.

Recently I was leading a girls group of high school students, and I heard one of them talk about how girls tend to change for a guy, but guys rarely change for a girl which I have to agree with; and this is because as women we are meant to submit. It is supposed to be a beautiful example and picture of Christ and the Church, but the enemy wants to try and prevent this from happening, so if he can manipulate and twist things, he will. But thank God we have already won the victory, and this life is but a glimpse. So when figuring out if a guy is for you, make sure not to compromise on whether he has a relationship with God or not.

Importance of Friendship

I think there is something to be said about being friends first before venturing into dating. I don't think you need to be "besties" right away or even hang out a lot. But there is definitely something special when you know you can be friends with the person you potentially will spend the rest of your life with. At the end of the day when life has gotten the best of you and your husband, you want to be able to call that person you are sleeping next to a friend.

Life is too short to waste time with someone who isn't, first and foremost, a friend.

And when it comes to dating, it is much easier getting to know someone you have already had in your life, whether just an acquaintance or friend of a friend; this can help give you a foundation from the start. I think it is great when couples meet and date right away, but it also puts pressure on the relationship before it is even a RELATIONSHIP. Dating and deciding whether you want to be with someone can be very tricky when you really don't know if you can be friends with the person. Time will tell, but so will friendship. When you are able to be friends first, you allow yourself to be exactly that, yourself! When you go into dating someone, not really having any idea about them, it is easier to hide and shy away.

Now I am not saying you can only date guys who are your friend first. So please don't start thinking about all of your guy friends as potential husband material because that could damage what you already have going with them. But if you head into something with the perspective as *we are just friends who want to get to know each other better,* then it can set you up for a win whether it works out or not because you are guarding your heart and his by not putting any kind of boxed-in preconceptions and thinking this guy is your husband from the start.

I have seen some beautiful relationships form out of people who had this perspective. I think it allows for more elements of surprise when you let go of how you think it should be. You hear people's love stories all the time: how they met, what their first date was, and when did they know they loved each other, etc. But those stories aren't love stories until after the fact. It isn't as romantic during the unfolding because you still don't know what is going on and if it will end in "happily ever after." But what is exciting and romantic are the unknowns that slowly are revealed through each conversation and each string of hope that this could be the one you choose to build your life with. Once you are married, you are bonded together till the end of time on this earth. So we have to choose wisely. And a friend, who may or may not be as attractive in 40 to 50 years as they once were, is who you will want to be by your side. Not someone who has become a stranger to you through most of your marriage because you never really took the time to get to know them, before you said, "I do".

Complicated

Relationships can be so complicated. Not only romantic relationships, but also friendships can be complicated between men and women. As I have gotten older and the more I have seen and experienced, men and women can only stay strictly friends when they are already taken or when there just really is not attraction between the two. But more often than not, one person always seems to be interested in the other.

One of my best friends, Melissa, has a situation with a guy friend who we will call "Robert." They work together and have gotten closer by spending more time together since she started working at the same company. They carpool to work together, text often, and plan hang outs always with other people included. They talk about what they want in their futures, share thoughts and dreams with one another. Robert told her that he isn't looking for a relationship right now, yet continues to act interested in her. He even tried kissing her one night after they had been out. She stopped him before he could go in for the kill, but it left Melissa confused. He says one thing and then does another. They talked about what happened, and he apologized. They agreed to stay just friends. But then he tries again a few weeks later but this time just to hold her hand. Again she is left confused. She is interested in him, but then again, she doesn't know if it is because she feels comfortable with him or if there is something more. She has been wracking her brain trying to figure out whether this is just her wanting and liking the attention or whether she actually sees potential with him.

Regardless of any of that, he has not expressed that he wants more out of the relationship. But his actions and words are not matching up. I have seen this and experienced this over and over again. Melissa is left distraught because she too has been in a similar situation once before. And now, not only does she have Robert being complicated; there is another guy who has actually been intentional in spending time with her and trying to get to know her. He is interested in her and makes it known. Now I don't know about you, but my friend and I have this in common, where we tend to go for the guys who are all wrong for us. The guys who aren't stepping up and aren't pursuing us. We go for the complicated, confusing, yet fun and mysterious ones who have us wracking our brains trying to figure out what to do. So who is in the wrong here... these guys or us girls?

I think both parties are. I think a guy needs to stick to what he says rather than being wishy-washy. If he just wants to be friends, then keep to boundaries and don't make moves that belong in the realm of a real relationship. And as for us girls, we need to stop hoping and thinking that these guys are going to come around. And even if they do come around, we shouldn't wait around for it to happen. What a waste of time!

I know it is fun and safe in a sense because nothing is going to come out of it, so you think, "Well why not?" But really, if we are honest with ourselves, we want the fairytale ending. I don't care who you are or what you are like, deep down every girl has a place in her heart for romance, surprise, and being swept off of her feet! And that is how God intended it. That is what He has planned for us if we just wait and let Him start writing our love story on our crisp, white pages. You don't want an old, used book where you cross out the names of the characters and replace them with yours and what's-his-name. God is the creator of the universe, yet we go and try to create our own love stories. Who do we think we are? (And mind you, I am writing this to myself, mostly).

We are the ones who make it complicated. We try to create something from nothing when God has our "everything." But God can't just hand it over to us because we want it. We have to fight for it. Just like He fought for us, we have to fight for a life with

Him. If we do not fight for that life, we will settle for "the rich guy who isn't the best guy, but at least we will be financially secure," or "the guy who is only really, ridiculously good looking, but has nothing else to offer," or "the guy who is so passive, he lets you control not only your relationship, but him as well"…leaving you feeling out of control since we weren't created for that kind of life. We all have the choice to settle or fight for what we have always wanted. So really when you look at it, black and white without any grey, we are the ones who complicate it. God already promised us a good future; don't you think that means a good husband, which will result in a good family? There isn't much more we can ask for when looking for love.

God is love, and God isn't complicated. When the right guy comes around, it won't be so complicated. It may be challenging, but not confusing. You will have the choice to move forward and fight for it or you can shut down, back off and settle for the next guy. I know it is hard. I know it is a lonely road. I know it can be confusing, but let's just make the choice to not complicate things. We need to focus on Jesus, the perfect bride groom, look for a man with His qualities and character, and if a guy doesn't have that, then move on quickly and cut our loses. Do not try to make something from nothing. Do not wait around, hoping and praying he is going to change, because he won't, at least not right now and not with you. And that has nothing to do with you nor does it mean that there is something wrong with you. It just means he isn't the right one. So don't waste your time. Then complicated can become simple, and simple brings you what you want and what you were created for. Simple is the equivalent to God's grace. It is simply receiving a gift from your Heavenly Father who wants the very best for you and is just waiting to give it to you.

10.

Be the Best You Can Be

I recently asked a married friend if there was one thing she could go back and tell her single self, what would it be? And she said to be content and as happy as you can be while single because it will only make married life that much better; simple advice, yet so profound.

How many times have we told ourselves, "Well I'll be happy one day when…" especially in regards to getting married, as if marriage is supposed to answer all our lifelong goals and problems. But if that were the case, how sad would our lives actually be? My married friend also mentioned that by not focusing on making her life all that it could be while single, it caused her to put more pressure on her now husband when they were dating. She said she wasn't fun to date because of it. She said that most guys would not have stayed with her and put up with the mess that she felt she was during the beginning of their relationship. Luckily she found a good one that loved her regardless and saw more to her than her current struggles. For some people, this is their story, but it doesn't work like that for everyone. I think my friend would agree that it would have been much better if she had learned beforehand that it wasn't her boyfriend's job to make her content, but it was, in fact, hers.

I encourage us all to do the same. I mean, if we are going to have to wait for the right man to come along and not settle we might as well be content and happy in the process. There are no downsides to doing so, but you will have to let go of some of the control; ultimately God is the one who can bring us to full contentment that is lasting and genuine. We are only truly content when we have surrendered everything to Jesus. And trust me, I tried to do things my own way for years, and it didn't really get me anywhere on my own. Some of you know exactly what I am talking about, and others of you may still be holding on to your own plans, trying to make things happen in your own strength. It can only last so long until everything comes crashing down. It isn't because God wants us to fail or be upset, but He knows what is best for us, and all we need to do is believe Him.

When we are able to be our best: confident, assured, and esteemed, that is when we are most attractive to everyone. People, including potential suitors, will flock to you, if you are authentic. When we are our best, we are happy and exude light, which only draws people in. The more we can live our lives with joy and happiness the sweeter life will be. Like the saying goes, "you can catch more bees with honey than you can vinegar." Now we are only trying to catch one, but which is sweeter, honey or vinegar?

Just Be You

The more you can be yourself, the better. I have found that the more confident and comfortable I have become in myself -

personality, physicality, and character - the more guys I have interested in me. I am not saying this in a conceited way, but it has taught me the value of confidence. I mean, even when looking for this quality in a man, it is so important. The less I have cared about what others think and just have been myself, the more I have grown. I now know my value rather than trying to prove myself to people and especially men. In the past I was always trying to be what they wanted me to be. I was constantly trying to be someone I wasn't and comparing myself to other girls wishing I could be different. But as soon as I realized who I am and how great I am, that was when guys came around. And then once I had more "options," I learned that I could say NO.

"No" was a word that I had to relearn when it came to men. I always felt I owed them something and that I was less than them. I am not sure if you have struggled in this area, but for me it was such a stronghold. I couldn't say no in the little things or the big. I never wanted to upset them or cause any frustration for them, so I would bend over backwards or worse, compromise myself. I would give parts of myself that were not intended for anyone else other than my husband. I gave too much of my heart rather than protecting it and guarding it.

But when you know who you are, you do not need to please people. Instead you look at your life as yours, and you offer it to God and not people. People will only get you so far, and people will always be capable of disappointing you. But God, He will never disappoint. He is the one we can trust above anyone, and He is the one who will carry us through the good and bad times.

I recognize that not everyone who reads this will know God. And I know I keep referring to Him and bringing it back to Him, but I do not know any other way to put things. If you are struggling, He is your answer. If you are lost, He will find you. If you are hurting, He will help you. The only true way to know who you are is by knowing Who you belong to, your Creator. He teaches you how much strength, courage, and value you have. It does not mean your life will be perfect or easy, I have actually found it to be quite the opposite the more I follow Him. But it is worth it.

11.

Freedom

How he treats you matters. There are too many women being verbally, sexually, and physically abused. Before you enter into a relationship with someone, and especially before you marry them, watch for red flags that may lead to bigger issues in the future. Red flags could be a bad temper or simply just putting you down in subtle ways. If he isn't respecting you, your body, mind and spirit, then it will not be the healthy relationship you desire. For decades women have taken a backseat to men, thinking that will help men feel stronger and better about them. But when a woman takes a stand for herself and what is right, it speaks volumes and attracts the right kind of man who will feel stronger and more of a man, having a woman like that by his side.

At times women have belittled themselves thinking that it is a humble position to take in life. To never think you are too pretty. To never think you are too great because heaven forbid you actually think highly of yourself. The lies we have been told from the generations before us have really messed with our heads and hearts. We become numb to the things that should make us feel the empowerment we are called to grab a hold of and take charge. Women are powerful - and that power can be used for our own selfish, manipulative motives or it can be used to strengthen the people around us. Confidence and assurance are contagious. When we rise up and become the powerful women we were created to be, we release other women to do the same and it continues to spread like wildfire. When we dream, it allows others to dream. Creativity is not created on its' own—it is a product of others' ideas catching fire from another's genius.

The beauty of life is living it freely. Free to be who we are, who we want to be, and enjoying the product and fruit of that. Too often we look at the rules and regulations that want to restrict and hold back the already bursting-at-the-seams light that is in us just waiting to make its appearance. So why do we do it to ourselves? Why do we hold back and hide the beauty inside of ourselves? We are afraid. Afraid to be adored and admired. Afraid of the attention that comes with showing our true beauty. But we long for it at the same time. How twisted is the human mind and heart. I think we are afraid because once we reach that point, there is no going back and with that comes pressure and expectations. I know for me, I am afraid that I will make a huge mistake and let people down. That they not only will see my strengths and the better parts of me, but they will also be able to see my weaknesses and faults. But what we don't realize is how it is even more beautiful to reach that potential while having weaknesses showing. Weaknesses are just as beautiful when they are accepted and nurtured into an opportunity to grow and be real and authentic.

Weaknesses and mistakes show humanity at its rawness and reminds us *Who* we need and *Who* we can depend on. Without weakness, there would be no reason to be in any relationship and especially one with Jesus. If we had everything all together and didn't need anyone, then what would be the point of spending time with people and giving and receiving love?

Let us be free. I challenge you today to take a stand, rise above, and start walking in your freedom. And do it every day. It doesn't just happen once or overnight, but walking in freedom is a choice every day. The more you choose it, the easier it becomes. But when you are walking in it, believe me, you will start attracting the right kind of man. Men who are confident and free themselves will come running to you and not be afraid or intimidated by you, but they will run alongside you cheering you on. This is how it is intended. Life not held back or restricted, but life that is filled with endless possibilities.

Red Flags

We just mentioned red flags in the last sections. Red flags are talked about so often when it comes to dating. Depending on where you are at in life and your perspective, it is tough to spot red flags. It is easy to compromise on certain things when you are not firm in your convictions and beliefs. I have done it many a time in the past. First it starts off small, and we convince ourselves that *he isn't that bad...I can get over that*. But those small compromises become bigger and bigger until we are dating someone who doesn't have the same morals and values at all.

When I was in my early twenties, I did this all the time. I let things slide on what actually mattered to me. I chose guys who were not on the same page as me at all. Hey, as long as they went to church and were cute, then I was willing to bend some rules. But I quickly and painfully learned that just wasn't going to cut it. I am still learning to spot out those red flags early on or even more so, just pay more attention to them. As soon as I see one now, which sometimes can take more than a few dates, I move on and don't let my heart and mind entertain the idea. This has been very helpful because I don't waste time, energy and feelings over someone who is not my future husband.

The way to spot out red flags is to know where you stand. Know where you stand when it comes to marriage, sex before marriage, your relationship with God, morals and values. Once you have these down and in concrete, you are able to know where you can go from there. It makes it easier not to waver in double mindedness. And in order to stick to these standards, you cannot get distracted by the way they may make you feel or the way they look. You may need to put feelings aside in order to really see the person in front of you. Does he want the same things as you? Do his actions align with his words?

Consistency in character is imperative when deciding if someone is right for you. Some guys know just what to say and later on you may find that they aren't the person they appeared to be. This is no fault of your own, but it can teach you for the next guy you meet. Being aware is so important, but this does not mean that you should read into everything that he says. I think as women we have a God-given instinct to spot out red flags in a potential partner. We just need to learn to tap into that and use it to our advantage and know when to let someone in and when to guard our hearts.

This instinct is not right all the time though. There have been times when I thought for sure that someone was right for me and was my possible future husband. But when I do look back, I see that that was just me wanting to believe it. It is a tough balance to learn, but I do believe we can master it, and it can save us from a lot of heartbreak.

Respect

Respect must first come from a respect for yourself before you can respect others. A lack of respect stems from feelings of unworthiness. If you feel you are not worth what you actually are, you will not see the worth and value of others. Men especially want respect. When a man does not know his worth and value, he will demand it from his spouse. But if he knows who he is and the value he has, he will respect others and in turn receive and accept the respect he is given. This is also true of love, but love cannot be fully experienced without respect going hand in hand with love. It is widely believed that women want love and men want respect, and it is as if they are equal for each gender.

It is sad but true that throughout history men have disrespected women. This happens because men are not dealing with their insecurities and issues. Men tend to dislike looking too deeply at why they are the way they are. This is a generalization, not all men are this way, but it can be very true for some men. Also it can be true for women, but stereotypically women are more in touch with their feelings. The worst part is that some women think that they can change this about a man and help them through their issues. But if a man does not want to deal with something, then he won't. It eventually boils over and can become a raging problem in his life. Their women will take the brunt of it and hope that things will change.

Now this issue of disrespect has another side to it as well. If a woman does not respect herself and she allows a man to disrespect her, then this is another tragedy that adds to the unhealthiness of a relationship. Women cannot be disrespected if they do not allow for it. It is so sad that in our world today there is so much physical and verbal abuse that takes place in many relationships and marriages. It usually stems from unhealthy patterns that were learned from parents as a child that gets passed down through the generations. But what is amazing is that we have a choice whether to break the generational curses that have been bestowed on us.

Men need respect. And if you are dating a guy who you have trouble respecting because of the way he may treat you or others, then that is a red flag, and you need to move on. You are not always going to find it easy to respect your man, especially if you are a more sassy woman like myself, but you know the difference between whether someone is respectable or not. It's like our mothers always said, "treat others the way you want to be treated."

It is much more simple than we make it. But I know how hard it can be when a relationship is already in too deep, and you don't know which way to go from there. But until you are married, you are not legally bound to someone, and it is much easier getting out of an unloving and disrespecting relationship.

12.

What Was the Point

In life we are constantly meeting new people. People come in and out of our lives whether it was for a brief 5 minutes in the aisle of a grocery store or whether it's for a few months or even for a few years. Sometimes it is for friendship, and other times we may date someone for a short period. I used to get so frustrated with God when I would meet someone I was interested in or would even go on a few dates with, and then it wouldn't work out. I would ask God, and myself, *Why? What was the point of that?* We may never fully know the answers to that question, but what we can do is walk away with some positive lessons or revelations that we did not have before.

For instance, I recently went on some dates and was getting to know someone for about two months. I knew he was planning on moving to New York to pursue acting, but we still decided to get to know one another. We clicked and were both interested, so we just went with it. I used to put so much pressure on dating that at this stage in my life I figured I would try not to over think anything and have fun. It worked out for the most part with the occasional freak-outs from him not calling every day. But with the dating relationship we had, I was able to find my voice. I went through years of my life not sharing how I felt or calling out behavior I didn't appreciate where I felt disrespected. But this time I would be different. And I was as vulnerable as I could be in the time that we had together, though I was still guarded with him because I knew he was leaving and ultimately knew he wasn't going to be my husband.

I could look at those two months as a waste of time or I could walk away with the lessons I had learned about myself. Also I found things about him that I liked and would want in a husband as well as other things I didn't. For me it was even a test to see where I was at; it had been over a year since the last person I actually liked and with this one I got to see where I had changed and where I still needed to grow. Not only all of that, but he challenged me to go after my dreams and to not be afraid which I had never had a guy really do before. Yes, I wish it could have worked out and who knows what would have happened if he hadn't moved. But everything works out the way it should, and I am happy I got to know him.

There have also been times when I have had an incredible time with a guy, and it is almost too "coupley," and it gets confusing. I still don't fully understand why these moments happen with these guys, and nothing ever comes from it, even though it so speaks to my heart's desire. But what I am realizing is that having these moments with someone who isn't my husband is only pointing me in the direction of my future husband in the sense that I am learning more and more of what I want in a man. And when I meet a man who possesses all of those qualities, from the big to the small, he will be much easier to spot out. Sometimes these moments with the ones who are not my husband have me wondering if they possibly are "him," but then when I think about it, I know in my heart that they aren't. Again it just points me back to what God has for me, which is everything and more. God isn't going to hold out on the man He has for us. He is going to surprise and shock us in the best way possible. So the point of all these fun, yet annoying encounters with all these guys who aren't *Mr. Right* are just bringing you closer to the real deal.

Give Yourself Time

With social pressures and our biological clocks ticking, we tend to worry about time. Most people want to be married by a certain age and some of us may already be past that age or quickly approaching it. Time and aging becomes our enemy as we wait "drowning" in our singleness. Yes, it is true that statistically we have a better chance of having children in our twenties, but more and more women are having children later on in their thirties and forties. But still some may have more trouble getting pregnant the longer they wait.

These facts can be overwhelming and confronting when you are still single, and there's really nothing you can do about it. We are to just wait for our *Prince Charming* to come and save us from the inevitable passing of time and dying of our eggs. But seriously though, Abraham's wife Sarah got pregnant with Isaac when she was old, like ninety years old kind of old. God can make miracles happen regardless of any circumstance.

We must be kind to ourselves when it comes to our timelines. It is not fair to compare your journey and life to someone else's because we are all so different and need different things at different times. I know it is hard not to compare when engagements, weddings and babies are all staring you in the face. I get it because I am there and everything in me wants to freak out about how I am quickly approaching thirty. Heaven forbid I get married in my thirties (eye roll). For me it has been a real fear of mine, but the longer I wait and the closer I get to turning thirty, the less I am worried about it. Why? Because what is the point in trying to control something I cannot control. What is the point of working myself up to the point of desperation where I could potentially make a big mistake with the wrong guy and waste even more time?

So take a deep breath and relax - everything is going to be all right. You won't die alone. And if you do end up waiting longer than expected or if you do happen to be someone who is called to singleness, God will be there to guide you through it. But if He has not told you that you are called to singleness, then I highly doubt you are. So don't worry, enjoy your life, and don't sell yourself short. It isn't a waste of time if you are using it wisely by bettering yourself, going on adventures and focusing on yourself and your relationship with God.

13.

Breaking a Bad Habit

Habits are formed over a course of time. They could be good habits like exercise, eating healthy, reading the Bible, etc. But we can also form bad habits. Habits are a series of behaviors that form a pattern and are not easily broken, especially when they are bad ones. We can take on habits from our parents and other family members, and a lot of times we don't even realize we have any. Many are harmless, like biting your nails, while others can be detrimental to our health and future.

We can form habits when it comes to dating and the guys that we choose, and in the way we treat people and the excuses we use. For me I have formed a habit of going for the bad boys. The charismatic types who are flirtatious and, though they are a lot of fun, they are the ones who usually, have drama following them.

The ones who make you wonder if you are the only girl for them or not, which most of the time you are not. These bad boys, when you are alone with them, make you feel like you are the only girl in the world, but as soon as other girls are around, you second-guess their loyalty to you, and your mistrust starts to seep in.

Now I know I am not the only girl who falls for these *bad boys,* and many of you can understand where I am coming from. I have rattled my brain trying to understand why we do it to ourselves and why do we continue in this bad habit over and over with a different guy. I understand where my bad habit stems from; I could blame it on my mother who had the same bad habit when she married my dad. I could blame my dad for being one of those "bad boys." I could blame all the guys who have been a part of forming my bad habit. Or I could just take the responsibility and realize this is a pattern in my life, so now how can I change it?

I have often questioned if I really do want to be in a relationship or if I am subconsciously choosing the ones who will never turn into something more serious because deep down, I am afraid and don't actually want to commit. Or…what I like to believe is that, yes, this is a habit in my life, but God has been protecting me from each one of these "bad boys" by not allowing me to be in a committed relationship with them. He knows what is best for me. God already knows who I am going to marry and when it will happen. He knows every detail of my love story. Maybe God is just waiting for me to kick this habit myself because He knows I can and I will. In fact, God believes more in us than we believe in ourselves.

We can do all the soul searching, reading, journaling, praying, and reading of the Bible we possibly can and still have this unending desire to be with someone who is not right for us. I think what it comes down to is this: Are we willing to break through our idea of what we want in a guy - *looks, personality, humor, etc* - and are we willing to receive who God has chosen for us? We ultimately make the decision, but God has someone in mind for us, so we can take the leap of faith and trust that God knows what He is doing.

We can keep coming up to the same mountain; rather than climbing it, we can keep walking around it until we have completely exhausted ourselves, requiring us to camp out at the base of the mountain until we are ready to do it all over again. I don't know about you, but I want to camp out and regain some energy so I can climb over that mountain, preferably with the man I am meant to be with.

We have all heard the saying, *there are plenty of fish in the sea.* And as cliché as it is, it is a cliché for a reason. It's true! If we just look around and realize that there are plenty of guys out there, maybe we would get better at choosing the right "fish." We don't need to get so hung up on one person and try to make something happen because we have slowly become more and more desperate, trying to grab onto someone who was never meant for us anyway.

Try and open your eyes to what's around you. I'm not saying go date any and everyone. But if you can change your perspective of being close-minded, someone unexpected may surprise you. Break your bad habit because you deserve it!

First Break the Cycle

Dating a "bad boy" or not, there still might be other bad habits in your life that you need to get rid of. Habits, these negative behaviors, cannot be taken out until a good habit is formed. It must be replaced with something. Just as if you were to give up coffee, cutting it cold turkey could only last so long. Now if you were to replace it with tea, another beverage or even another "ritual," it will last.

Other mountains to face in kicking a bad habit are shame and guilt. If you are feeling guilty, that can potentially lead to shame if it is not dealt with healthily. Shame only keeps you where you are at and does not allow you to get past the bad habit or sin you have committed. Shame and guilt keep us hiding from not only ourselves but others as well. The more shame we feel, the more we push people away and only hurt ourselves in the long run. Shame and guilt do not come from God. Many people think that being a

Christian means you feel bad about everything. Many non-believers think that God makes you feel guilty. What God will do is convict someone of something they have done wrong, but that is different. Condemnation comes from feeling guilty then ashamed. I dealt with both ugly monsters most of my growing up and even into becoming an adult. I would constantly tell myself that this is not from God, but that the enemy wants me to feel this way. Often times it did not help because I could not shake the feelings that were so intense. And to be honest, I'm not sure when God fully lifted those feelings off of me. But it was probably when I better understood His unconditional, never-ending love for me.

I used to feel guilty for feeling guilty. I could not shake it. It was a part of my DNA it seemed like. So God had to give me a new DNA, a better one - His. And He did. With enough time, prayer, and fervency, God healed me and broke the chains that were holding me back. I still have to choose not to let the feeling of guilt overtake me and turn into shame, but He equipped me to do so, so it wasn't as hard as it had been before. You may be reading this and not believe in God. But whether you do or don't, we all can struggle in this area. You could have "inherited" it from your parents, and it may be plaguing you right now. But trust me, you do not have to carry that burden. The Bible tells us to cast our cares on Jesus. He is the only one who can carry that much weight and relieve you of it. It sounds weird, but if you just ask Jesus to do it, then He will. What do you have to lose!

So How Do We Do It

How do we stop going for the wrong ones and start going towards the right one? I think it is as simple as a decision. I think we must decide that we are done with mediocre and start believing for the very best. Set the bar high and don't let emotions and impatience get the best of you. Every time you have a negative thought about never meeting the right guy and how you are going to be single the rest of your life, shut yourself up. Pull yourself together and know that those are lies from the enemy. If God has given you the desire to be married, then He will fulfill His promise to you. It may not be when you want it to be; it may be much later in life than you imagined. But being single doesn't mean you have to sit around, twirling your thumbs, waiting for Prince Charming. You can explore, travel, set goals and achieve them. You can start a business, volunteer, do a missions trip whenever you want. You have so much more freedom than someone who is married and especially someone who has children.

Seize the day and stop living for what's in the future or what is behind you. There is too much to squeeze out of life than just waiting for your life to happen to you. You can live your dreams now. Obviously it will look different, but the more you focus on your purpose and live it out, the more you will be in a position to meet Mr. Right. And the more you do that, the less you will care about whether or not that guy you have had your eye on pays attention to you or not. Because you will know how incredible you are and how much of a fool he is to not pursue you. Then it won't matter because he wasn't the right one for you anyway.

I think we put way too much pressure on ourselves, and we worry about things we have no control over. I know this because I have done it myself. But I am finding out more and more that life is short, and there is no use in wasting time worrying and being frustrated. This is easier said than done, but with the help of the Holy Spirit, it is possible. Once we understand and look at life as a whole, we are able to do things we want to now. We don't have to wait for a husband and children to live out our dreams. There are things that God has for us to do now while we are waiting. And most of life is waiting anyway, so we should probably get used to it and learn to enjoy in the midst of it all!

Obsession

What is it with many women obsessing over men? Not just any men, but the wrong men. They let it steal their joy and happiness all because one guy won't give them the attention they so desperately want. I have not only seen this, but I have experienced it as well. As young girls, we obsessed over boy bands and celebrities such as The Backstreet Boys, N*SYNC, and nowadays, Justin Beiber. Even from the start, we long to devote ourselves to a man. As we "mature" we move on from unattainable pop stars to the cute, star quarter back of the football team or the badass skater boy who skips class. Whatever our type was it just continues until we meet our true Prince Charming and live happily ever after. But as women we move from one guy to the next hoping this is IT. Whatever IT is. Or some of us can't actually move on to the next guy because we have become so fixated on one guy who is just some guy who we have made into THE guy. But after multiple heartbreaks (with the same, "some guy") we continue to have empty hope that will eventually lead to nothing.

I don't think this is our fault that as women to want something to work out with a guy who we are interested in. God has called us to relationship and to become one with a man when it is the right person and the right time. But too often, women run themselves rampant trying to make something work. I often find myself saying, "Oh I would date 'so-and-so' if he were like this" or "He is great, but would be even better if he were like that." But really, he is never going to be this, that or the other if he isn't already like that or in the process of becoming like that. Did you follow that?

This want and need to change things can be healthy in the right settings, but when it comes to people, it cannot be done. It is a waste of time and energy. People will change if they want to. But still, there is something else in us when we become so obsessed on one person who isn't even right for us. I think there is something more within that we can't even comprehend or realize. Honestly, we are meant to "obsess" (meditate) over the things of God. We are wired for it. But the enemy can easily grab hold of that within us if we are not careful and use it to distract us with things that we cannot do anything about anyways.

Imagine if women were to take the brain space, time and energy they use to obsess over men, and use it for good - those women could cure cancer or change poverty. Those are extremes, but seriously women could do some pretty incredible world changing things if they would just stop thinking about things that don't matter and put their energy towards things that do.

I remember my mom, whenever my dad would go out for the day on his motorcycle or was out late, would spend her time trying to figure out where he was and what he was doing. She didn't trust him and with good reason, but I was always amazed at the stories or possible realities she would come up with on where and what my dad was doing. It got even worse when they were going through a divorce, and she would speculate on who he was dating and if he was hiding money from her. The stories I would hear were like a script to a movie. My mom has always been very creative, and I just wonder if what she actually thought was going on with my dad was true or not. If anything, it showed me that my mom was very intelligent; but what a waste of intelligence and creativity. It can drain a person when obsessing over the wrong things. That obsession then becomes anxiety, which leads to so many other problems and issues.

Depression can seep in and take over someone's life where they can't eat, sleep or function at a normal level and all because of focusing on the wrong things. Our minds are very powerful. They can make us or break us; they can build health or tear us down. We have the choice on where we allow our minds to go and what we allow our minds to do. Easier said than done, but with prayer and wanting to change, a lot can be achieved. Let's use our brains for greater things than obsessing over things we cannot change.

Obsession doesn't come from nowhere though. Depending on your past, this kind of behavior stems from somewhere. A lot of times, manipulation, whether from you or someone else, can lead to obsession. Or if you have been abused in any way: verbally, mentally, emotionally or physically. Abuse alters a person and can make them act in strange and unhealthy ways. Obsessive patterns are made even worse by not trusting God. When people are relying on themselves more than God that is when it gets dangerous. You can start playing God and thinking that if you do not control the situation, no one else will. Obsession can also stem from control issues, which stem from other problems. When someone has experienced trauma or an unstable upbringing, this can cause trust and control issues. It makes sense though. When a person has had no stability, they try to grasp on to anything that looks somewhat stable. So men for instance, or a relationship even if it is unhealthy, is easy to hold on for dear life.

Unfortunately this behavior is so common, and many people don't even see the reason behind their actions because it is too painful to look at. If you are someone who is facing this, I suggest talking to a professional counselor. They can help you filter through your experiences and help you overcome any strongholds in this area, and of course prayer helps tremendously. You have to be diligent in fighting it and keep pressing on because it is a tough habit to break. But you can gain freedom in it. I know I have. It was hard, but it was worth it - I had to fight and fall many times. It took me making a lot of the same mistakes to finally get it to click.

You may not have struggled in this area, maybe you know someone who has, and the best advice I can give is to keep loving them and speaking truth to them. People who obsess and have these issues are very broken. They come from a lot of hurt, confusion, and abuse that really takes a toll on them. It takes years to bounce back from such experiences. So try to be patient and understanding even if you don't know what it is like. Be a non-judging ear to listen. Most of the time they don't even need your advice because they already know what they are doing wrong. But they just need someone to listen and to encourage them and speak life into them. Eventually with time and God on their side, He will see them through, as long as the person wants the help and wants to change. You can't help anyone who won't help themselves first.

14.

Unhappiness and Despair

Sometimes when we stop and actually have time to think, we realize all that is missing in our lives. When the chaotic schedules that beckon for our attention finally come to a halt for a few days, we can really reflect and look at our lives. The emptiness that might be there hovering over us like a dark cloud that can easily bring about a storm if we are not careful. I have had one of those weeks. I have had time to evaluate my life and see that there is not much to show for it tangibly. The last year and a half I have dedicated my life to ministry school and what I have really gotten is a mended heart and a deeper relationship with Jesus. It has been priceless.

But I have also realized the lack of resources in my life. The lack of a husband, a lack of a job or career that I love, a lack of resource to do the things I want to, a lack of a family. Now it is easy for me to go there and start to feel sorry for myself or I can choose to look at all I do have. I am living in one of the most beautiful places in the world (Sydney, Australia), I am from the "promised land" (Southern California), I get to fully submerse myself into the things of God and intentionally put my life "on hold" to grow and learn. I am blessed. So much of me though is crying out in despair because as the people around me are falling in love left and right, having babies, getting great opportunities - I find myself at a loss.

Now I know God can do impossible things. I have seen it with my own eyes. But as I wait, I slowly find myself less and less happy with what I have. I have so many dreams that are yet to be fulfilled, and sometimes I wonder when they will ever happen. It makes me want to take a stand, and grab my life by the horns and take off running. I don't mean run away, but run towards all that He has promised me. Take a stand and grab hold of some things I have been waiting for.

We have to let our fears and doubts turn into something greater that will spur us on to the greatness that is ahead! The enemy wants to get us in this waiting season of singleness. He wants to tell us lies and get us to believe that what he is saying is real. He will tell you that to compare yourself to everyone around you. He will tell you that you aren't good enough. He will tell you that you will always be single. He will tell you that you aren't ready. He will tell you everything and anything but the truth. So anytime you hear anything of the sort, remember who is saying it to you and grab life by the horns and run for it. Run to your Heavenly Father who will remind you of all that HE has for you. He will remind you of how beautiful you are. He will remind you of your righteousness. He will remind you of the opportunities He has for you. His unconditional love will envelop you, and you will be able to find happiness and hope again.

Loneliness

Loneliness is defined as being "affected with, characterized by, or causing a depressing feeling of being alone; lonesome. Lonesome is defined as depressed or sad" because of the lack of friends, companionship, etc. I think we have all felt lonely at times. That aching pain deep within our souls, the longing for companionship with another human being, someone to love and cherish us for all that we are; a person who will care for us and protect us from any trouble that may come our way. Feelings of loneliness cloud our hearts and minds and weigh us down until we feel as if we would rather die than be alone. Or at least it makes us crawl back into bed and not wake up for a long time.

Loneliness slowly creeps in and steals us of any joy or happiness we may have once had. We start thinking that we will never be happy again and the only way we possibly will ever be happy is if someone finally chooses to love us.

But even then, once the excitement of relationship slowly starts to wear off, we are back to feeling lonely again, even if that person is right next to us with their arm wrapped around our shoulders. That is because there is a deeper loneliness within all of us that longs to be in a close relationship with Jesus Christ. He is the only true and lasting fix to the problem of that deep loneliness. The only one who can reach to the depths of our souls and fill in the void that aches within our hearts. Until we let Him in and let Him have our whole heart, we continue to fill our lives with empty imitations.

But if we are patient and wait for the true Redeemer of our souls to pursue us like we were intended to be, He far exceeds any expectations we once had. Once our True Love, Jesus Christ, is placed in our lives and hearts in His rightful place, our first love, He can then add to it our earthly husband. If he is the right man for you, he will reflect Jesus through his actions and character.

I am not going to lie; it is a long process for God to fill the voids you may have in your heart and to take full ownership of your love. Sometimes it takes a lifetime, sometimes it takes a few months, but no matter what, you can rest in the fact that He will pursue you always, even after He has won you over. He isn't a typical guy who says he is going to call and never does. He will keep calling until you answer. If you are feeling lonely, the best things you can do is write or pray to Him, Jesus, and ask Him to send the Holy Spirit to comfort you. Let Him wrap His strong but gentle arms around you so tightly that there is no way for you to feel alone. Ask the Holy Spirit to speak to you and assure you that He is with you and loves you. He is just waiting to sweep you off your feet like never before. He is the Creator of romance and companionship. The last thing He wants is for you to feel alone.

You may not feel His presence right away. You may go through phases of feeling alone even when having a close relationship with God. I go through waves of feeling alone, and sometimes it is really painful. The enemy wants us to feel alone and stay in that place of loneliness. He would love it if you believed that you would always be alone. And honestly sometimes I want to sit in that and believe it because somehow it seems easier at times because it can be painful to have hope. At least if I believed that I would always be alone, I could accept it and move on with my life, never to hope for something more. But how sad does that sound. It would quickly turn into depression, and my life would be meaningless and empty. I have felt that in the past, complete emptiness, and it is a scary place to be.

I believe God allows us to feel lonely sometimes so we realize our need for Him. It also helps us relate to others who may be in the same spot. I am learning to embrace these feelings of loneliness that sometimes creep in because it reminds me to press into God even more. It reminds me that I am human, and I can't always be so strong and try to keep it together. No, I have feelings and emotions, and it is hard being "alone." It is even harder when everyone else around you seems to not be alone.

Let's face it - it is hard being single. It is even harder being single when the majority of your friends are not. You feel like no one understands you and your struggle because they are past it already. You feel like you have no one to talk to about it, no one to lean on and encourage you because you feel ashamed that you are struggling with it. At least that is how I feel at times. Sometimes I feel so strong and independent; other times I feel like I can't go on like this anymore because when will my turn come? When will I get to share my life with someone?

But I want to reassure you that if you are feeling lonely or if you have in the past, you aren't alone in feeling that way. Pretty much everyone deals with it at some point in their life. Just know that it won't last forever and try to be patient in the wait. God will be faithful, and He will come through for you just when you need it. Don't let the enemy take over and feed you lies; spot the lies and speak truth to yourself. Help is on the way!

15.

Do What YOU Want

I think as Christians we become way too concerned about what everyone else wants for us. Christian or not, everyone is susceptible to it. But as I get older and learn more, I am realizing how important it is to do what you want and have fun! Now I'm not saying go and do whatever you want if it is immoral and harmful, obviously. But if you want to go move somewhere, do it! If you want to get a tattoo, do it! If you want to go away for a weekend, do it! If you want a dog, get one!

Obviously in all these things, you must be responsible and do what is best for you. And one thing may not be good for another. But if you have prayed about it and have peace, then I don't see what is wrong in doing what you want. God wants us to be happy.

I know for me I have struggled with this. I have cared way too much about what other people think and other people's opinions. I have been afraid of making a wrong turn or decision. But ultimately God has the final say, and if He doesn't want you to do something, He will step in and make it known.

I really believe we think too highly of ourselves and think that we need to control our lives as much as we do. God is bigger than our seemingly increasing control issues. He makes a way where there is no way. He moves mountains and calms storms. So at the end of the day, all we need to do is trust Him and enjoy the fullness of a free life that Jesus paid for a long time ago. He is just waiting for you to go away with Him and not be fazed by the monotony of life that so many get swept away with.

People will be offended by your choices more often than not. Just remember it is usually an indicator that you are doing something right. When there is opposition, there is usually position on the other side of that decision. Position in your life can look like a job, a relationship, a salary, a trip, etc. It can look like something tangible or something spiritual that can only be seen on the other side of eternity. Either way it is a win somewhere along the way!

During the time when I first started to write this book, I found myself at one of those crossroads. My life was becoming stagnant, and I needed to do something about it. I had been waiting and waiting for a husband, hoping that was what was going to make my life "begin." But when it didn't "begin," I knew something needed to change, and it wasn't me finding a relationship. I started thinking about what I wanted to do with my life since all of my previous plans had failed. I revisited an old dream of going to grad school to become a Marriage and Family Therapist. It is something I had planned on doing previously and even was accepted into the program when I first graduated with my Bachelors in Psychology. I had asked for guidance in this decision from leaders and members of my church, and they encouraged me to do so. It was a good move at the time, and it would eventually lead to a potential job for me with a nonprofit organization established through the church. It sounded like a dream come true. But as time went on God reminded me of another dream He had put on my heart of moving to Sydney, Australia and attending Bible College there.

I spent almost a year being confused on what to do. But I was so scared about what others thought was right for me rather than listening to myself, and what God was speaking to me. I pursued the grad program yet again. I still remember the day I received the acceptance letter. I opened it at work with my co-workers watching me, and I was so disappointed that I was accepted yet again. Most people would be overjoyed with the opportunity, but all I was hoping for was that I would not get in, so I had a clear yes or no about moving across the world to attend Bible college. My sheer disappointment should have told me then and there that I didn't want to go and that it was okay I didn't want to go. But I knew I would be disappointing many people in my decision.

I kept wrestling with the two options. Nothing was making sense, and I didn't know what to do. One night I was even spiritually attacked in my sleep over it. I kept hearing a voice tell me *you can't go to Australia*. It kept repeating over and over. I couldn't get rid of it for a while, and I felt so much agony and pain. I thought it was God saying this to me until I learned that God doesn't inflict pain like that. And that is when it clicked that it was the enemy trying to get in my head once again. Still not knowing what to do, three weeks leading up to the grad program, I was to start paying. But I could not get myself to pay; I didn't have peace about it at all. That was when I called up my leader and let her know that I just couldn't do it. She was disappointed. Just the thing I was trying to avoid. I proceeded to tell her that I am still thinking of going to the bible college in Australia, and again she did not really agree with my decision. This pained me because I valued her opinion of me more than anyone. But I couldn't ignore what God was putting on my heart even though I wasn't sure at the time it was God at all.

I am so thankful for that experience because it taught me to value obeying God over pleasing people. It was a big lesson for me, and one that has shaped many of my decisions since. I had numerous people disagree with me moving to Australia for two years. They thought I could learn everything I was going to learn by staying where I was. And I believe if I had stayed, God would have taught me similar things, just in a different way. But I am so glad that I did move because it helped me grow much quicker than I could have imagined. It has been challenging and still is. But as I wrap up my Bible college experience here in Australia, I would not trade it for anything. God knows what He is doing, and He wants us to do what we want. But He will put it on our hearts at the right time for the right purpose. It may not make sense at first, but when we are obedient and step out, it is amazing what He will do in our lives.

Key to Happiness

I have figured out the key to happiness; the thing we all hope for and dream of. It is to not worry! Imagine that, not worrying about who you will marry, what you will do with your life, where you will live, how many kids you will have, etc. The way we do not worry is by trusting God. If we can trust Him with our future, then nothing can hold us back. Obviously this is easier said than done like most everything. Probably the hardest thing I have ever had to do, over and over, is to let go and trust God. But once we do, freedom settles in, and our hearts are enlarged and softened and ready to receive whatever God's next gift is.

Trust does not happen overnight. It is a journey that can take much longer than we ever expected it would. But God works with us and takes us step by step, slowly but surely.

In Philipians 4:6-7 (NLT) it says, "Don't worry about anything; instead, pray about everything. Tell God what you need, and thank him for all He has done. Then you will experience God's peace, which exceeds anything we can understand. His peace will guard your hearts and minds as you live in Christ Jesus."

I think, as women, we constantly want to figure out life and problem solve. We like to know where we are headed and whom we are headed with. But what is the fun in that when we know everything that will take place in our lives? God loves to surprise us! He loves to romance us, and romance is filled with mystery. The mystery of God is what draws us to Him. He intrigues us because we do not fully know Him yet, and we continue to want more of Him. Being happy is found in the contentment of the mystery. Being more than okay with the unknowns. Rather than letting them discourage us, when we can allow them to excite us and see it as an adventure with our Savior, it changes everything about our lives.

Life is meant to be LIVED. And living looks like not holding back, not shying away because of what is not yet seen, but grabbing life at its full potential and not letting go of the promises God has placed in our hearts. It is hard to do in the culture that we live in. Our cultural norm is to have five and ten year plans with goals and deadlines. Our culture labels us by what job we do rather than who we are and the thoughts and dreams we have. We live in a day and age where status and money are held in high regard. People live to work rather than work to live. I know not everyone is like the status quo, but majority and popular belief is that whoever can get to the top first wins. Not just with money though, we also get it according to our relationship status. And since meeting the man of our dreams is not exactly in our control, how is that fair? Unfortunately, we cannot change the cultural norms and perceptions, but we can choose how to live our lives.

And what if we decide not to live like the rest of the world? What if we start dreaming and doing? What if we start changing the way in which our world works, and we say what is good and acceptable for us? Let us break through the boxes that have been placed on us that we are "supposed" to live in the confines of. Let us push the borders. Do what you love and what makes you happy whether it makes sense to others or not. But what truly makes YOU happy. Do it for you and not for anyone else because at the end of the day, you are left with just you and your life, no one to tell you how to live and what to do.

Start Dreaming

"A dream is a wish your heart makes," sang Cinderella. Unfortunately, so many of us have left dreams up to fairytales. But we were destined to live out a fairytale. We are royalty in the kingdom of Heaven. I recognize that for some of you this may be the first time you are hearing that you are royalty. But it is true. You are a daughter of the KING - Jesus Christ. Your inheritance is the kingdom of God, meaning everything here on earth as it is in heaven. This might sound crazy to you, but imagine living, knowing you are royalty. It may change your life, and if it hasn't, it should.

Being royalty means that nothing is off-limits. This gives you the right and freedom to dream a bigger dream. I understand that many of you reading this may come from a tough background where dreaming was never an option. Your life may have been more poverty than royalty. And I apologize if this is hard for you to read or understand. But I won't apologize for calling you royalty because you were born for it, and God intended for you to have all the riches in the world whether that has happened for you financially or not.

God has hopes and dreams for you, but He can only make them happen once you start to dream yourself. Do not feel unworthy or unqualified because God does not *call the qualified, but He qualifies the called.* And you, my friend, are called. You are called for greatness whether your life looks like it right now or not. It may take time for you to see it, possibly longer than you thought. But like it says in Philippians 1:6, "And I am certain that God, who began the good work within you, will continue his work until it is finally finished on the day when Christ Jesus returns."

Dreams are what keep us going - they are the fuel to our fire. Without that fire, we are dull, burnt out, and dried up logs waiting for someone else to ignite us. Let's get it started and bring the spark that can cause a forest fire of hopes, dreams, and never-ending excitement for the unknown.

When we understand and have this revelation that we are royalty, and it can cause us to start dreaming, we then have vision. Without dreams and visions for our lives, we will go nowhere. We will start to look for dreams in a man rather than dream of our future husband. There is a difference. Just a few years ago, I tried to plan my life around a guy who was never going to be my husband. I was trying to find vision for my life through his life. I was so desperate to have him as mine that I started to lose my own dreams and justify and compromise the vision God had given me. It is a very dangerous place to be, and if we are not aware, we can easily lose who we are. ROYALTY.

God can only start where your dreams start, so dream far beyond where you think you can go and He will take you further than you ever thought you could. This includes the dreaming of your future husband. And I am not talking about dreaming about the cute guy next store, and if God doesn't make it happen, then you are upset with Him. But dream of the kind of man you want and what your life could look like with him by your side. What will you bring to God's kingdom together? What will your family dynamic be? Where will you live? But hold these dreams loosely because God has the final say and may call you to other things as a family, but at least you are starting with the foundation of what is to come.

16.

Limitless

It always amazes me to hear people's stories, especially their stories of how they met their spouse. I am sure you have heard it before, "It happens when you least expect it." As much as that saying used to frustrate me, the more I am realizing it is true. I have not experienced it yet, but I have seen it happen to many others. As much as we want to figure out our lives and how things will unfold, the more God wants to surprise us.

God always works outside of what we think is logical and makes sense. Though he is a logical God, at the end of the day, we just don't understand his logic most of the time. But recently I really feel God has been putting on my heart that He is limitless. Limitless in the way He does things. We may think we have a good idea of how our lives should go, especially in the area of waiting for our love story to begin. But what I am learning is that whatever you think should happen, expect it will probably not be like that at all, not if it is God-breathed.

That doesn't mean it won't be just as amazing. Honestly it will be more amazing and incredible than you even can imagine or realize. He has the best plan for you, and He cares about the longings of your heart. He will bring up longings that you forgot you even had. He will awaken things in your heart and spirit that you didn't even know were there. He loves to break through the boxes and boundaries we put Him in. He wants more for you than you want for yourself. So when you are frustrated with how long it is taking to begin, don't lose courage or hope. Remember He has bigger dreams and desires for you than you could ever fathom.

It may be taking longer than you hoped because He is continuing to stretch you and make room for what is ahead. For me, my life was so small before - I was always so scared and held tightly to what I had. I didn't want to let go of MY dreams and what I wanted. But God slowly started softening my heart and slowly started asking me to do things or give up things I never thought I would be able to. It wasn't to be mean or hurtful, but it was for my own benefit. I needed to let go of some things and let go of myself in order for Him to start stretching me and my capacity to love - not only others, but myself in particular.

It reminds me of this quote by C.S. Lewis that a friend shared with me:

"Imagine yourself as a living house. God comes in to rebuild that house. At first, perhaps, you can understand what He is doing. He is getting the drains right and stopping the leaks in the roof and so on; you knew that those jobs needed doing and so you are not surprised. But presently He starts knocking the house about in a way that hurts abominably and does not seem to make any sense. What on earth is He up to? The explanation is that He is building quite a different house from the one you thought of - throwing out a new wing here, putting on an extra floor there, running up towers, making courtyards. You thought you were being made into a decent little cottage: but He is building a palace. He intends to come and live in it Himself."

This is the way in which He works. We think we know what He wants for our life, and we picture the white picket fence and all; it sounds like a dream, it sounds perfect. And there He goes and starts building so much more than we ever thought possible. Our limitless God wants us to keep expanding and creating room for Him, which will only make more room for everything else, He has in-store for us.

It can be scary and painful at times, but it will be so worth it when we have the furniture all moved in and we wake up in the morning with the sun spilling through our window and all seems right in the world. Of course, that is after we have made our coffee or our future husband has brought coffee to us while still in bed. Now that is a dream! Those will be the moments we understand everything we had to go through before we could be given the promise we so desperately longed for.

All These Things Will Be Added

Matthew 6:33 (ESV) says, "But seek first the kingdom of God and His righteousness, and all these things will be added to you."

If you want to know the answer on how to have your dreams fulfilled, including your dream of falling in love, getting married, etc. this verse is it. Seek God's kingdom. Maybe you don't know what that looks like or means. I didn't know at first. I thought I was doing that, and here I am still single. But what I have realized is that it does not happen overnight. And it doesn't mean seek His Kingdom every once in awhile or just on Sundays. Seek it every day; seek it every minute of every day.

Now you may be wondering what that looks like on a practical level. Obviously we can't be spending hours upon hours praying in our bedrooms with worship music on and candles lit for some atmosphere. Though that would be nice! But what it does look like is choosing His will before ours or anyone else's. It looks like choosing to put your faith in Him in all seasons and circumstances. It looks like building His church in whatever capacity it looks like for you, even if that is attending every Sunday until you feel prompted to do more. Or it looks like not going to church for a season and you inviting the Holy Spirit into your day from the most menial of tasks to the most complicated.

Seeking His righteousness looks like living an authentic life; an authentic life that is living above reproach. One that is seeking to be more like Him and less like ourselves or more like our redeemed selves. It is a life worth following: one filled with encouragement, love and respect.

Seeking His Kingdom first looks like choosing Jesus and His will for your life above a man. Any man that asks you to choose him over God's calling for your life is not the right one. He should be so close to Jesus that he would never ask you to do that, but he would support you in it. This is the only way to build a healthy foundation for life and any relationship. It won't last or be what you wanted otherwise.

The good news is that when you choose God's kingdom and purposes, then all these things will be added. It may not be tangible at first, the tangible form of a man. Like I said, it may take time. But everything that God does while you wait: the beauty He will show you, not only around you but in you, the little miracles He will provide, the quiet whispers to your heart that will uplift you. All these things add to make a fulfilling life, and the idea of a husband becomes less and less important to you. The focus becomes the bigger picture when your eyes are focused on the things of eternity.

It used to scare me to stop focusing on a relationship because I thought that is what I needed to do in order to obtain one. But don't you know that the harder you try to hold on to something the easier it is to slip right out of your hand. But when we hold tightly to the things of Heaven, you just receive more and more of it. The tangible dreams of a husband and family and all the things that come with it will come to be, but what will you do in the meantime? Who will you be when you meet him?

17.

Is It Love?

How do you know when you are in love with someone? Is it butterflies in your stomach? Do you know right away? And what if you love someone who cannot reciprocate the same love?

In the past there were many guys I thought I was in love with, but as I got older and wiser, I realized I was just infatuated with them. Infatuation means *to inspire or possess with a foolish or unreasoning passion, as of love.* I remember being ridiculous when it came to a guy I was "in love" with. I completely made these guys into something they, in reality, weren't. I dreamt up how they could be, instead of who they actually were. I saw their potential rather than their present selves. I read into little comments or actions towards me, thinking it was more than it really was. I think girls can attest to doing this in some form or another, at some point in their life. Looking back, it is so silly to think about, but then it was my reality.

[THEN - when I thought I was in love]

But now I find myself loving someone who is not capable of loving me back. And I don't know if it is just right now or ever. So what do I do with that? He shares his feelings with me and makes it sound like he cares just the same as I do for him. But he has been heartbroken in the past and still struggles with it whether he will admit it or not. He and I dated for a brief time over a year ago, yet we still find ourselves drawn to each other in most social settings with friends. We still kiss occasionally, which I definitely don't condone if I am being honest. Things are still not completely over between us. I want them to be, but for some reason they are not. This last time we made the mistake of locking lips; I couldn't help but realize that I do in fact love him. I have loved him this whole time. But he has broken my heart many times while in his brokenhearted stupor. This has caused me much turmoil, thinking I must be an idiot and crazy for still loving him and caring about him and even wanting to be with him if he finally got it together! This has given me much fear too because my parents had a rough relationship that ended in divorce. My mother was hopelessly devoted to my abusive, cheating father, which caused her much regression in her life. Not that she was fully whole even before they got together. But regardless, I am my mother's daughter and I have her same heart. And if I am not careful, I could easily be taken out by the wrong guy. And I would say that has already happened with this particular individual. I do feel more together again then I had before, but it has been a slow recovery process.

Still though, after all I have been through with him, all the tears, pain, rejection, and heartbreak, for some reason I still love him. I talked to a friend of mine about this once, and he told me that it must be some gift God has given me with people. I am resilient when it comes to relationships with people. They can hurt me, offend me all they want, and I will still love and forgive them. I may not trust them like I once had, and I definitely set boundaries.

But I do believe God has given me such a gift, and when used correctly, it can be very powerful. But in situations like this one, it can be taken advantage of very easily. I loved that my friend shared this with me because I had never looked at it as a gift and always looked at it as a flaw.

I am sure you have many gifts that you may view as a flaw, problem or issue like I have. But that is what I love about God. He uses everything for good.

Romans 8:28 (NLT):

"And we know that God causes everything to work together for good to those who love God and are called according to his purpose for them."

Whatever our shortcomings are, they are actually a gift when we surrender them to God and let Him transform them into something He can use for good. I believe that God will use my ability to love and forgive people for good. He already has in some ways. Most times I don't see the reason for it, but I know He does, and I just need to trust that.

[NOW]

Looking back at the relationship I had with this boy, I see that I did love him. I saw him how God sees him. Like I said before, this is a gift, being able to see the potential in people and loving them for who they truly are in Christ. I saw him, not for all of the mistakes he made and pain he caused me, but for the heart he has despite all his downfalls. But what I have come to realize and see now, now that I am out of this unhealthy relationship is that I was holding onto something that was never going to be. It was never going to be because he and I have two very different lives, hopes, and dreams. And even if we were meant to be going in the same direction, we definitely weren't. God was calling me to a different way of life, and I had to let go of the idea of a relationship with him if I was going to obey God and pursue what God has for me.

I was blinded by potentials and hopes, which were not a bad thing, but in the end God has my life written out and knows whom I am meant to marry, and He was not going to let me go off on my own. It took me a year and a half of being invested into something that was never going to be and a flight to Australia to start Bible College in order for me to move on. I had to be physically removed from the situation in order to see clearly and grow in some areas of my heart to understand and remember again who I am and whose I am. God loves us too much to let certain relationships happen and end in marriage.

All the times you or I have felt rejected because something has not worked out, has just been God protecting us all along. It is hard to see it that way when we are in the midst of it. But if we are truly seeking God and in relationship with Him, He is not going to let us settle in life. He loves us too much to let us get married to the wrong guy. And even though at the time of this relationship I really did believe I was in love with him, I do not regret anything that happened between us because it brought me to where I am now. Everything always happens for a reason, and again God always works everything out for good. Once we really believe that, beyond just knowing it, that is when God can do something in our lives and possibly bring the right guy to cross our path. We will never fully understand reasons why, but we have to trust that God has his purpose in it all, and that is all we need to know.

When You Know, You Know

"When you know, you know" is what they say. I have heard it time and time again when I have begged the question, "How do you know he is the right one?" And that is the response I would get. As frustrated as it would leave me, I think it is true. When the combination of the right timing and the right person collide into you, I think you quite possibly know. After you know, it is a decision that needs to be made, from then on, to stick with them. But it seems like when you are ready to start writing your love story with someone, it won't be perfect, but it will be right.

You'll know when you know because you won't feel uneasy or have constant doubts about your relationship or questioning if they are right for you. You will know because he will treat you how you always wanted to be treated. You will know because he will bring the best out of you. He will challenge you and encourage you. He will fight for you no matter what. He will be a gentleman and honor and value you. You will know he is the right one when he opens his heart up to you. You will know he is the right one when he calls you when he says he will. You will know when you know because he won't ask you to give up your dreams for him, but he will champion you in them. And you will know because he will make you laugh.

Too often we give all these excuses and reasons to ourselves about why that someone might be our potential husband, all to later find out he was just another imitation of the dream that God has put in our hearts. Why do we do this to ourselves? We get our hopes up and try to make a guy into the man of our dreams when he doesn't even come close to the real thing. We slowly start to settle into these compromises that begin to shape our lives. It is a scary thing to lose a dream, especially when it is our own doing.

As women of God we need to let go of our own timing and trust that God has it sorted for us. More often than not, do I hear women who are married now say, "If I had only known what God had in store for me, I would have enjoyed my waiting season so much more." As unnatural and hard as it is, we need to get to a place where we see our lives from the perspective of what is to come. Now this will take faith, A LOT of faith. But if you and I can muster it, we could enjoy the time we do have and suck the life out of it! Every last drop, and really start living for something bigger than our wedding day, which is a long, happy life, filled with love and adventure.

Life is too short and we have too much to learn and experience then to sit around waiting for Prince Charming to come and "rescue" us from ourselves. Let's create our lives rather than letting lost hopes and dreams shape us. Bring those dreams and hopes up; let them encourage you, not discourage you. If you can start to conquer some of your dreams now, then God will only give you more dreams. He is the limitless God who has way more to give us than we ever ask for. Your best days are ahead of you, but don't miss out on today.

You are probably thinking, well how will I know when I know? And I wish I had a clear answer for you. But I am continually learning that only time will tell with matters of the heart. I wish there was a clear cut formula to all of this and I could give you some major words of wisdom here, but all I know is that you will know when you know. I have heard so many stories of how people came to be a couple and then decide to spend the rest of their lives with each other, and each one is unique. You never know when it is going to click and fall into place. Some may have more of a battle than others at the start of their relationship. Some take years to figure it out.

There have been times when some of my girl friends, who in my eyes should have given up on a guy a long time ago, end up happily together with them only six months to a year down the road. I used to think I had it all figured out. But I just keep learning I actually don't know much at all. I know what I want, and I won't settle for less. I know how I don't want a relationship to start, but at the end of the day it really isn't up to me. We never really know when it is going to work out and when it isn't. And again, that is the risk we take in the quest for a lasting relationship. I think each experience I have had in this area with a guy has helped me learn and grow.

I have been heartbroken and hurt, but I have found hope again. My heart has been restored, and it hasn't been from me searching for another guy to fill that space. But it has been me walking it out with God and wrestling with Him about it. But He knows. I may not know as much as I thought I did, but I think that is what growing up is. It is realizing you don't know as much as you thought you did and having the humility to admit it.

I still believe though that when I do meet my "Prince Charming," I will know he is the right one. It won't be coming from me, but the Holy Spirit will give me the peace I need to move forward in the relationship or not. I think a lot of times we forget that the Holy Spirit wants to direct us even in this area of our lives. He is not separate from our love life, but He is right there in the middle of it, waiting for us to invite Him in. He will speak to you about a man if you let Him.

He will remind you of dreams you have long forgotten about in this area of romance. He will gently nudge you if you are making a mistake. He will tell you when to pull back and when to go. He doesn't want us to figure this out on our own. It is such a big commitment to marry someone so why would we keep the Holy Spirit out of it? We may be afraid to hear what He has to say if it is not the right guy for us. It is hard to let go of someone you see a possible future with, but maybe your future is better off with the man who God has for you.

Fast Break

A few months ago I decided I was not going to date for 6 months. It was just after my twenty-seventh birthday, and I had just gone on a date with someone a few weeks before. I thought that it could actually go somewhere until I saw who he really was. He isn't a bad guy whatsoever. Honestly he is one of the better ones I have ever been interested in. But though he is a good guy, but he just wasn't confident and secure in himself. That is probably one of the most unattractive qualities in a person. When someone is constantly seeking approval, it gets exhausting because that puts a lot of pressure on you. This challenges me to be more confident and secure in who I am so that I can have a healthy relationship where the pressure is not on the other person.

But anyways, enough of my ramble, I say all of this to tell you that it just got me to the point where I was done. I was done with dating or being interested in all the wrong ones. Not wrong in the sense of bad, but wrong for me. They all have been wrong for me, hence why I have not had a boyfriend. I once had a guy friend say to me that I act like I am too precious. He quickly apologized, clarifying that I am precious. But it had me thinking after. Sometimes I can act like I am perhaps "too good" for some guys.

But honestly, I never mean it like that. I do believe though that we are precious. If God has been protecting me all of these years and not allowing me to get into a relationship with the wrong guy, then yeah, I would say I am precious. And so are you.

In Matthew 7:6 (NIV) it says "Do not give dogs what is sacred; do not throw your pearls to pigs. If you do, they may trample them under their feet, and turn and tear you to pieces." I am not calling all guys pigs here, especially not my friend who said that to me, but we do need to be careful that we are holding ourselves to a high regard in the sense of not giving ourselves to men who do not deserve even our time of day. You know the ones, and if you are the way that I was and seem to attract these "types," learn from me and run as fast as you can.

Because I have had my fair share of the wrong ones, I am taking a break from dating. Not even a friendly, innocent coffee date. Of course during this time I have not even been asked on any. It is like when you make such vows, God actually listens to you and makes it easier for you when really I almost want to be tempted to test myself. During this break I decided to fast this month, no sugar for the month of September. And I am fasting for my husband that he would come into my life soon. Fasting for our future relationship and the way it will unfold. I also have started a journal written to my future husband. And I have to tell you, I feel so silly writing it most of the time. I mean I am writing to a man I don't even know yet, and I am writing such personal things with the expectation that we will be close enough when I give it to him that the things I have written won't be weird. It is like having a wedding board on Pinterest when you aren't even in a relationship, and you have it set on private, so no one else will see it because that would be weird to plan a wedding without a groom (guilty!). I do these things not because I am obsessed with getting married, which I definitely had been a few years back. But I believe there is power in these acts of preparation. I am making room for possibilities and when the time comes, I will have the room and be ready, practically and spiritually.

Maybe for you this is all too girly. Maybe you have never been the type of girl who has dreamt about her wedding since she was a little girl. But either way, there are ways to prepare yourself or make room in your life for what is ahead. I think fasting is so powerful. If you do not know about fasting, I suggest you read a book on it such as *Fasting* by Jentezen Franklin or ask your pastor. But for me, during this time of fasting from dating and from sugar, I have been feeling like I am Esther in the Bible having her six months of beauty treatments preparing for the king. I feel like I am preparing for my husband during this time, and it has honestly been better than I expected. The Holy Spirit is showing me how much I have grown in this area of singleness and how I don't have to feel lonely or sad about it, but I can actually embrace it and get to know Him better.

Singleness is such a gift. I know I have said it before, but I will keep on saying it until you too have this revelation because it will change how you see this time in your life. You may not stop hoping and wanting to be married, but that is a good thing. Without that hope and desire, it won't keep the dream alive that is the promise of your future husband and future family.

18.

You Are More Than Enough

Have you ever felt not good enough? What about, have you ever felt not good enough for a particular guy? I have. I think most people have struggled with this in one way or another. But it just simply isn't true. I think any guy that makes you feel that way is not the right one. It could be through an insecurity of yours that needs to come out. Women in particular struggle with this sense that they are not good enough. We try and try to be better, do better, feel better, and we come up short. But that is okay because God is the one who makes us enough. I know it sounds cheesy sometimes, but if you do not understand this truth yet, I am telling you from the depths of my soul that we women are MORE than enough because He makes us enough. We can relax and take a deep breath. We can stop trying and start living. If you aren't feeling like enough for someone then move on from them. Move on to someone who makes you feel like you are more than enough. Someone who brings the best out of you and knows how good he has it to be with you. If you haven't found that yet, then he isn't the right one. Don't settle just because you think that you will never find someone who will treat you this way. He is out there. It may take longer than you had hoped or expected, but rather wait now than pay later. And yes I am talking about divorce fees.

Be committed to making the right decision when it comes to a man. Don't be afraid to say no to someone who asks you out because you think no one else will ever ask you. Don't be afraid to move on to someone else or even just remain single because you think it is impossible to meet someone. I know this is all easier said than done, and I am not intending to frustrate you. But these are our goals for living a single life that is full of contentment, satisfaction, and fulfillment. Sometimes it seems impossible for those words to describe singleness, but it is possible. I am living in that now, as crazy as it sounds. I, myself, am in shock over it. I never thought I would reach this newfound sense of wholeness while being so single. I have no prospects at the moment, not even a crush. I should be hopeless and desperate, at least that is what the world says, but I am not. I am happy. Life isn't easy, but life isn't meant to be easy. It is meant to be full of challenges that will shape us into the person we are meant to be. Challenges strengthen our character and sift what needs to be taken out for us to live the full life we were intended to live. Don't despise your days of singleness because they will flash before your eyes if you are not careful, and you won't have gotten everything you needed while in this season.

Remember it is a season, and seasons don't last forever; once one ends another begins. Before you know it, you will be married with kids, and you will miss the days when you only had to look after yourself. So enjoy yourself! Learn as much as you can while you can and get as prepared as you can before it is time to be joined with the man of your dreams.

Insecurities Are a Killer

We all have insecurities. Men and women cannot escape the torment that insecurities sometimes bring. We try to hide them, run from them, and then there they are again coming right at us face-first for a head-on collision. Why can't we get away from them? Where do they come from? Do we even realize what they actually are? Insecurities can get the best of us if we let them. They can rule us; mold us into something that we aren't. They can hide our potential to the point we can't even see what's really there underneath it all.

Insecurities can haunt us from past experiences, our family dynamics, or lies that we have believed along the way. These ugly killers can keep repeating themselves not only in our current lives and relationships, but they can be passed down from generation to generation. We can feel like we are suffocating in our weaknesses and our comparison to others. We look at others thinking they have it all together when in fact they are probably worse off than us, but they have learned to mask it better.

We currently might be the most insecure generation because of the culture we are living in with selfies, social media now being a platform, and the superficiality that we cannot get away from. Everything in us screams out that we are insecure. For most of us, it comes from how we were raised and the troubles we have faced. Women have it the worst, with our bodies being objectified and only valued according to how we look to a man. It is sad and disgusting. But we also have the power to live above this. We can choose whether or not we are going to sit in those insecurities or if we will rise above and step out of them like we are meant to.

Insecurities make us shrink back. They breed fear and exhaust us; they are where the enemy would love to keep us. He would love us to stay miserable and insecure in our single days. He would love to lengthen them and cause us to believe that they will never end. Insecurities attract the wrong kind of attention and the wrong kind of man. When we are freed from them, then we are unstoppable. We start living the life we were meant to. We stop holding back, and we start moving forward without any reservations. We stop living afraid, and we start running ahead in life. We start to birth new things when we kill insecurities rather than letting them kill us.

How do we kill insecurities? We don't give them the attention they seek. We speak truth into them, and they slowly start to diminish with each word proclaimed over them. We don't believe the lies, we hold onto the promise, and we keep pushing forward. Even when it doesn't feel like they are dying, we keep proclaiming and believing until they are eventually silenced.

Regrets

Could have, should have, would have? I have had so many thoughts when it comes to previous "relationships" or guys that I liked where I thought *if I had only known I wouldn't have said this or done that.* And I used to think, *if I hadn't made that mistake, we might have been a couple and been married by now.* But none of it is true. I am a firm believer that everything happens for a reason, and the serendipity of it all will be the thing that brings a relationship about. Serendipity is a fancy, romantic word for the right place at the right time. A chance meeting, a coincident - I think not! More than serendipity, God's sovereignty is more powerful than our "mistakes." Remember He works all things together for good. So any regrets you may have, you can let them go and not worry because He will surprise you with the man and plan He has already worked out for you.

And if you are meant to be with someone you feel you have messed things up with, nothing is impossible. When it is the right person for you, that you can build a lasting relationship with, then nothing can get in the way of that. I think when we have regrets like this we are not trusting God. But when you fully trust Him with your life, then it is easier for you to let go of your so-called losses and walk away in confidence that there is a better plan for you.

Giving power to regret will not benefit you or anyone else. There is so much power in looking ahead and not behind. The enemy doesn't know what to do with us when we look away from our mistakes and really live out our new creation lives we have been given. What will you do with all the free headspace you will have by giving up wasted thoughts of regret? You are a force to be reckoned with and have a higher purpose and calling than spending your life waiting around for a guy who should be right alongside of you and not behind you.

Regrets keep you stuck in shame and guilt and can put you in a funk that is hard to get out of. Living in the past doesn't do anyone any good. People who live dwelling in the past are unhappy and lost. I have definitely been there before, and it isn't easy living like that. It will take faith to step out and move past it, letting go of any mistakes you feel you have made. But life is full of mistakes, some more consequential than others, and the only things you can do are learn from them and use them to help you propel forward.

Fear Is a Real Thing

Fear can be quite crippling in any area of life. But there is a real fear of never getting married that all single girls experience at some point in their lives. Our biological clock ticks on as we age, and everyone around us is getting into relationships, engaged, married, and having babies. And there we are, still alone, no one to call our own. It sounds so sad. And it definitely can be. I know some pretty incredible women who are doing big things with their life, still single, and still waiting for their man to appear.

When I think of their lives, I am encouraged, but I am also frustrated for them. Why hasn't it happened for them yet? Why hasn't it happened for me yet? When will it happen? So many questions with no answers in sight. But again, singleness is a journey like anything in life. And we have to just keep moving forward without letting those longings in our heart get the best of us in a negative sense. It is easy to grow in discontentment. But I know married women who still struggle with discontentment. They may not be discontent with their husbands, but there will always be something in your life you can get down about. If it isn't one thing, it is another, if you let it!

What a blessing and opportunity we have to take this time while we are "alone" and grow in our contentment while it isn't affecting someone else that we really care about. I know it is annoying at times, and we like to think that a man and marriage is going to fix everything. But I am sure once we are married with a family, we will know exactly what I am talking about. We only get one life that is measured by years, months, and minutes, and if we are not careful, we can easily watch them slip on by if we are not squeezing every drop of joy and contentment out of them.

Fear will get us nowhere; it is a dead-end road that will stop us in our tracks. But when we face it and move past it, we can start to live out the life we want. The more we can radiate our true selves, not bound by fear the easier it will be to attract the man of our dreams, attract the job of our dreams, and attract the life of our dreams. The enemy would love it if we would just remain fearful that we will forever be alone, never to find love we so desire. He would love it if we would remain paralyzed and overanalyze every move we make. Fear is his weapon, but we have truth. We have the God of the impossible on our side.

These incredible women I mentioned earlier have been waiting for their promise of a man for almost twenty years more than me. This is humbling and also puts things into perspective. They have chosen God's will for their lives over anything else. They are confident, bold women who love Jesus with all their hearts. This doesn't mean they don't still hope and wait and maybe even feel discouraged and sad at times. I am sure they do. But they do not sit around wallowing in what hasn't happened. They pick themselves up everyday with their head held high and go after their God given purpose.

19.

Real Intimacy

Being single isn't easy. Being in a relationship isn't easy. Life goes through its ups and downs, and all we can do is go along for the ride while learning the most out of each moment we are given. Everyone's journey looks different especially in this area of singleness. For some women they are given the gift of a man and relationship early on in life, and through that relationship God teaches them how much He loves them through their man's affection. For others, such as myself, God wants my relationship with Him to be as full as possible before He will let any other man love me and let me love another man. I have been so jealous of the "lucky" ones who have been blessed with their husbands earlier on in life. But I am learning that I too am lucky for being single at this age and this stage of my journey. God wants me to be fully in love with Him first. He wants ALL of my heart before He will allow another man to have any part of my heart.

It has been challenging and so difficult to give all of my heart to God. I have compared Him to other men in my life who have all disappointed me in one-way or another. My dad was the first to break my heart, and from there I allowed others to have that right when it never belonged to them. I would have done anything for my dad, and he slowly, but surely ripped my heart to shreds over the years through mistreatment and unrealistic expectations from me as his daughter. After that experience, it sent me into a spiral of throwing myself at any guy who would give me the time of day. I was so fearful of any male interaction that I usually had to self-medicate through alcohol just to cope with the nervousness I felt around them. This usually ended in being used and devalued to a mere body with no emotions or voice to tell them to stop before it was too late. My behavior eventually changed once I started on a journey of trying to love myself and mend my own broken heart with the occasional surrender to God when I couldn't take it anymore.

Through this process of trying to change myself, I made small feats and began to transform. But I could only get myself so far until I hit another wall or made the mistake of drinking too much again and doing something I regretted. I recommitted my life to Jesus I don't know how many times until I found a church that I loved and wanted to commit myself to, still not fully understanding I needed to commit myself to Jesus and not just His church. That went well for a while, and on the outside I seemed to be doing much better. I wasn't making the same mistakes with guys that I had been making before. I was starting to feel much better about myself, but I still wasn't whole yet.

My life took a huge turn when the enemy deceived me through the cute church boy I've referenced throughout this book. During this time I was swept up in the possibilities of the relationship actually having a chance of going somewhere because we at least had the same beliefs, or at least I thought we did. God still was calling for all of my heart, but I ignored Him and paid more attention to what this church boy was calling me for, and it wasn't my heart. I kept distracting myself with the possibility of my dream coming true of having a husband in this boy. Until months went by, and I realized we didn't want the same things after all. Instead of accepting it and moving on, I kept trying to fix it. I wanted it to work even though I was hurting myself in the process. I was left heartbroken again and it wasn't just one big heartbreak. It was heartbreak after heartbreak because I let him keep calling me back to him when he was bored or horny (sorry for being "vulgar," but not all "church boys" are as innocent as they come across). Like I said before, he didn't want my heart, but he wanted my body. And I let him, not all of it, but part of it, kind of like how I would only give God parts of my heart and not all of it.

And here I am, two years later from that heartbreak, and I am still struggling to give God ALL of my heart. I thought I had been, but the last year has been a process of me being in a season of wanting more intimacy with God and not knowing why I am not getting it. Until this last week when I had a break down that was the start of a breakthrough. I was completely overwhelmed by God's love for me and for people when talking to some friends about His love. I knew I was due for a break down or big cry because it had been a long time, and I had been feeling so full of emotion yet having no way to express it. I couldn't even really put words to it. And then there it was, an ocean of emotion that led to waves of tears that wouldn't stop once they started.

I went home from the conversation and couldn't stop crying. I went in the shower to hide my tears from my housemates because I wasn't ready to talk. I felt like my heart was literally trying to escape me as God was gently trying to take it from me, that last part that I had been so desperately trying to hold onto for this past year. It was painful, yet beautiful and oh so necessary. God knew what He was doing, and I know the timing was just right as it usually is. Since this night of tearful cleansing, I have felt lighter; but even better than that, I have realized what has been going on with me over the past couple years. God has been trying to get my attention. He has been slowly tugging at my heart and tenderly trying to take it piece by piece, so He could have all of it. I now know that I won't be finding my husband until God has all of me.

It has taken me longer than I would have hoped it would. But looking back at the many heartbreaks that I have experienced and struggled with over the years, it makes sense that it would be such a challenge. It isn't easy trusting anyone with your heart, even God, when you have been so hurt and mistreated in the past. There is the fear of it happening again that paralyzes us from handing it over without a fight. But what's so amazing is that God fights even harder to take our hearts than we are fighting to keep it. And He is even gentler than we are in the process. We stumble and grip so tightly, holding on for dear life as if that is what will save us. But we learn that it is the surrender that saves us, mostly from ourselves.

Experiencing all of this, I am learning what intimacy looks like. It has been a long journey and process learning intimacy, and I am still learning. But I had a moment with God while worshipping Him the night I had my breakdown (or break through, whichever way you want to look at it). I felt my heartbeat and I realized my heartbeat is the same as His. When we love Him and align ourselves and our dreams with His, we actually have the same heartbeat. In that moment, I understood what experiencing intimacy looks like. It isn't something sexual, but it is actually knowing one another so well that you know what makes their heart tick: what they're passionate about, what they love, and who they truly are. And I understood in that moment that I do have authentic intimacy with God, and it felt like nothing else I have ever experienced.

All these years I have thought I needed a relationship, my future husband, to know what love is and to experience intimacy, until I started to see that Jesus had been pursuing me all this time. He was patiently waiting for me to look into His eyes rather than looking around into others' eyes for something they could never give me. I am so confident that God is the one who will give me this sense of fulfillment when it comes to love more than any man ever could.

I believe for every single one of us (no pun intended ha) until we fully allow Him to have all of us, all of our hearts - fears, dreams, hopes, struggles- we won't be able to experience and be given the gift of a husband the way we want it to be. This isn't because He wants us to be perfect beforehand or because He is mean, but He is so jealous for us. He wants all of you, but only because He loves you so much. He wants you to be fully free and have the kind of life where you are able to walk in full confidence of who you are in Him. He really does know what He is doing ladies, as frustrating as it can be at times. And the struggle is real. It isn't easy to commit to this relationship with God. Even though God is so trustworthy, it doesn't really make it any easier. We have had experiences that have either built up walls within us or created fears that are crippling us, and we don't even know it. But that is where God works best; He breaks walls and melts away fear. He is not limited to the role in which we think He fits best. He is many things, to many people. He is not just the love of our life, but He is also an adoring Heavenly Father who doesn't even compare to our earthly fathers. He is protective and cherishes you, and He loves each of us uniquely. What makes your heart sing may not make mine feel anything at all and vice versa. And that is exactly the beauty of God. He can love many in many different ways!

Purity

Purity is not virginity or never having been touched in a sexual way. Purity is not being wholesome and clean; it is a state of the heart and mind. It is having good thoughts towards the opposite sex that are not taking you down a path of lust and sexual desire. Now don't get me wrong, having sexual desire is a good thing. It is God-given, but when it is awakened before it's time, it can be devastating to your wellbeing and health (physically, mentally, emotionally, and spiritually).

Purity is a gift from God that aligns us to Him. It is a trust and security between Him and you. We are born into this world as innocent and pure babies; we are weak and fragile and need to be cared for as these newborns. I believe those same characteristics are still how God sees us today. He doesn't care what we have done; He just sees us white as snow and pure as can be. Holy Spirit helps us keep our purity intact when life comes at us from all directions with its temptations and frustrations.

Our purity is a gift that we are to protect so that we can pass the gift on to our future spouse. Now I am speaking to you about this subject as a "born again virgin." If you didn't know that was possible, I believe it definitely is. I have made many mistakes in this area of staying *pure*. Out of my impatience, insecurity, and low self-esteem came my relentless desire to be approved by someone of the opposite sex. I had a skewed view of what intimacy was. I only knew of intimacy as the world knows it, through sexual acts. Because I could not be intimate by sharing what was on my heart and what my thoughts were, I gave my body instead. My "purity" quickly ran out, and I had nothing left to give by the time I realized what I had done.

But by the grace of God and through his love for me, He has set me free from the belief that I have to give my body first to be intimate and to find the "love" that I thought I wanted. But God arrested my heart and showed me that there is another way of intimacy, a greater way that is safer and more freeing than I ever thought possible. I believe our intimacy with God is a reflection of how our intimacy with our spouse will be. Sex within marriage is freeing and the most secure, it is a place where a husband and wife are able to share their heart's desires without fear or condemnation. This is how God intended intimacy and sexuality, and purity is the weapon against sexual immorality. It is a weapon against heartbreak, against abuse, against destruction to a person's spirit. Purity is one of the strongest weapons against the enemy.

Staying pure is not only not having sex or sexual acts with someone outside of marriage. Other sexual immorality is lust, pornography, and masturbation (when done with the wrong intent). I think these are more common for Christian singles than actual sexual acts with others outside of marriage. In today's society especially, pornography is much more common and not looked at as wrong to the world's standards, and same goes with masturbation which obviously comes with pornography usually. In the Christian world these subjects can be very hush-hush and not brought to the light.

The other presumption is that only men struggle with such things which is not true at all. I have had female friends within the Christian circle who have struggled with pornography. And I myself have struggled with masturbation. Now I tell you this in hopes that it will help free someone who may be feeling guilty of such an act of "sin." What upsets me is that it is not talked about as much as it should be. I think the reason many Christian women struggle with it is because it is looked down on with such disgust. I have had friends who have been so distraught hearing of women doing such a thing, and at the moment I knew I could not tell anyone with such a view that I masturbate. Not until one of my friends confessed to me about her own struggles, I then shared too. This brought to my attention that it is much more common than people think, and it is a bigger issue than we realize.

For the longest time I did not feel guilty about it or bad about masturbating. I wasn't doing it as often as I was when I first started as a teenager. I first started out of curiosity when some of my non-Christian friends talked about it. I did not realize the damage I was doing and the stronghold I was giving the enemy because I later did become addicted to it in one season of my life. I knew it was wrong, but I could not break away from the behavior. During this season of my life, I now realize why it was such an addiction. I was using it to make myself feel more attractive because at the time I was very insecure. I was moderately depressed, not feeling good enough, hating my job and where my life was at. I was in the thick of struggling with being single and desperately wanting a man. I felt extremely lonely during this time so all of that was weighing down on me, and so I used masturbation to help me feel better. It was always a quick fix for me, and I justified my action.

I have researched and read many articles on Christian perspectives on masturbating, and I found so many different answers. Most of the views brought up that the actual behavior of masturbating is not the sin and the issue, but the issue is the potential to lust because of the images that may be in the mind during or if porn is involved. But for me it was never an issue with porn or even lust. What I did find when I researched Christian perspectives on the matter is that masturbation is a very selfish act. Sex was created in order to give to your spouse and vice-verse, and since masturbating is by yourself, for your own selfish, temporary gain, it was not how God intended sex to be. But with saying that, what is a girl to do when she is still single and expected not to have any sort of sexual activity?

In one of my classes at Bible college my friend asked one of our teachers, who is highly reputable in her Biblical knowledge, her thoughts on masturbation. To my surprise, she never said it was wrong. What she did say was that it depends on the reason behind it. Obviously lust and pornography are not okay because that is bringing images to your mind that are immoral. But the respected teacher said that if she had a student come to her and tell her that he masturbated instead of sleeping with his girlfriend, she would much prefer him to do that than the latter. This had me really thinking because I myself have been on a journey of trying to work out what I think about it. I know that previously when I was addicted to masturbating, it was a major issue, and I see that now. But if I do it occasionally now, it is never for any reason other than feeling horny, for lack of a better term. I know this is uncomfortable reading this, and believe me, it is much more uncomfortable for me writing it and thinking of you reading it. But I just feel this topic is rarely talked about, and it causes many people such guilt and shame where I don't think God wants us to feel that way.

I believe the biggest things we need to remember when talking about this subject is if you are engaging in masturbation, why do you do it? If you truly believe that it is not for unhealthy reasons, filling a void, or even pulling you away from God, I do not think there is anything wrong with it. Now if it becomes an addiction, then that is another story. But what I do suggest is to ask a friend to be your accountability partner, female of course, to talk it through with you so you are always aware of where you are at with it.

Not too long ago I really did think it was completely wrong. But I have prayed about it so much and asked God to help me not do it. But I always end up engaging in the act once again. Until I feel God is really telling me that it is wrong or if I believe it is becoming a problem, then my stance on it is that it is not a sin. Plus I think it is funny that we are more accepting of guys masturbating than we are girls. The common belief is that males are more sexually charged than females, and I have to disagree. Not just from my own personal experience, but talking to other females on this subject, it is a lot more common than people think. And purity does not mean you never have sexual feelings. I think women especially tend to feel guilty because there has been a popular lie that we are supposed to not feel anything and remain a perfect virgin, and then next minute when we get married, we need to be these sexual beings. It just isn't fair.

Where we can challenge ourselves though is staying pure in heart and mind. So like we talked about above, eliminating any sort of lust because that is sin. Lust towards another person, so thoughts of having sex or anything of the sort with someone, is not okay. Jesus makes it clear that when we do that, it is like we are acting it out and have committing the sin (Matthew 5:27-30). You may not struggle with this issue in particular, but maybe there is something else you may need God to redeem and purify within your heart and life. Or maybe you know someone struggling in this area, and you have judged him or her in the past. Sin is sin at the end of the day, and we all are on a journey to keep our purity intact. I believe no matter what we have or haven't done in regards to sexual sin or purity in general, whether it was through an act or thought, we have all fallen short of what God has called us to. But the good news is, we have Jesus, and He heals and redeems those broken parts in our hearts. He is waiting with open arms to heal us of any type of addictions, struggles, and dependencies.

He wants to be intimate with us in the purist sense of the word. He wants genuine love and devotion on our part; He wants us to trust Him so we can be free and pure like He created us to be. He does not want us to feel shame and guilt. He wants us to feel protected and safe. So go to Him wherever you are at on your purity journey and ask for His guidance and help. I know I am still on it, and I may never know or have the best answer, but I am doing my best and walking it out with Him, and that is all I can do.

Protection

As women we want to feel protected. We want to feel safe and secure, and sometimes we want that comfort in the form of a man's arms. A man's strong arms wrapped around you, close to his chest, protected from any harm that has the potential of hurting you. We long for this kind of protection and safety. For years I wanted a man to rescue me from myself and from the agony I felt of being alone, being single. It wasn't until a few years of maturing and learning that I saw the real reason behind my singleness lasting for so long. It wasn't that there was something wrong with me, and it wasn't because I wasn't beautiful or worth a boy's time of day. It was God protecting me. I didn't realize it at first. I felt terrible about myself and single situation; and it plagued me. But once I had the revelation that is was all quite the opposite and that God cared that much about me that He wasn't just going to give me to any guy. He was going to wait for the right man and the right time before giving me away.

God was longing to have intimacy with me and have my whole heart before He was going to let anyone else have part of it. He wants ALL of us before He lets anyone else have any of our hearts. It is actually a beautiful thing to have such a strong Man cherish you so much that He protects you from all of the potential disasters that men could parade through your life. And when I say parade, I mean the kind of guys who just walks on by, capturing all of your attention without even looking back. We have all been there, paid attention to the wrong guys for way too long, thinking that we don't deserve them when in reality they don't deserve us.

We, as women have it so twisted sometimes. We don't see reality, but we make up these things in our head that tell us we are inadequate and not worth it, but it just isn't true. And we know where it comes from, our pasts, our upbringings, but ultimately from Satan himself. He hates beauty because it is competition with him. That's why he hates you because you are beautiful. You steal God's attention, and he doesn't like that, so he tries to steal ours. But once we realize that God is protecting us from potential heartbreak, potential distraction and destruction, and potential settling, we can celebrate what He is saving us from. He is our rescuer! We don't need a man to rescue us because God has already been doing so. He fills that need for us to be saved and looked after. So then we can go on, move on, and not worry about whether a boy likes us or not.

Once we have a sense and understanding of how safe we really are in God's arms, we begin to breathe a bit easier, we loosen up and become more ourselves, and we stop trying to be something we're not. That is when we become our most attractive selves, not only to boys, but also to people in general. This is when we start attracting God's favor and blessing in our lives. And once we are walking out our victory, we don't worry so much about our single selves and we start focusing on the things that matter. We begin to walk, with our heads held high, where no man can tear us down or hold us back. We are free to look forward with purpose and confidence and show the world who we really are, unapologetically.

Ladies, walk with your head held high because you have God, the creator of everything, protecting you. So don't be sad that it hasn't worked out with that guy from church or the guy from down the hall. God has you covered, and He has the best for you. Believe it and watch it happen!

20.

Everyone but Me

As I am getting older, it seems like everyone is getting engaged, married and having babies. Every week there are new couples emerging around me and dream proposals. And here I am...still single. It is seemingly getting harder and harder to find a man, a potential husband. And yet I still have to wait and trust that God has someone for me when everything in me wants to freak out.

Most days I feel confident in my singleness, and I know that it won't last much longer, whatever "longer" looks like. Other days, usually when I am PMSing, I feel like I will never get married, that I am not desirable, and life is hopeless. Obviously I know none of that to be true, but in those moments of doubt I want to stay and live in them. I almost feel more justified thinking that way because when you look at the facts, it would make sense that I would never get married. I am only saying this because I have never been in a proper boyfriend/girlfriend relationship. I normally don't notice my singleness that much because I choose not to pay attention. But when you are faced with it daily via social media, that little annoying voice of doubt creeps in and starts nagging at me about when it will be my turn.

I am sharing this with you all so you know that I am not always positive about this subject and season. Most of what I write in here is for me and to encourage myself while hopefully helping you as well. This is real, trying to navigate life single and being content while still looking forward to the future. Still I wonder how it will ever happen. How am I going to meet this amazing man who adores me? Even when I find him, will it be all that I've ever wanted? These are the questions and doubts I am having in this moment. But I know they will pass because ultimately I know the truth. And the truth is the enemy wants us to believe these lies. He wants us to be afraid and doubt what God has for us. He wants us to compare ourselves to others. He wants us to feel inadequate and not worth it.

But we are worth it. We are worth the chase, worth the pursuit, but if we don't believe it, no one else will either. The best we can do while everyone else around us is the happiest they have ever been, is to be happy with them. We will reap what we sow in due time. And if we can be happy now for others, we will eventually reap that same love and excitement they are feeling.

Perspective is so important when we are feeling this way. In reality not everyone is married or in a relationship; it just seems that way because we tend to notice what others have that we don't. But there are a lot more single people out there than we may notice. So we are not the only ones left alone. It is hard though if the majority of your friends are not single, which is my case. I tend to fill my life with busyness to avoid feeling alone. Like last night for instance, I was feeling desperate to find plans for my Friday night. It is rare for me to not have plans, so then when I don't, I get anxious thinking of being alone at home on a Friday night. I know it is so silly, but it was how I was feeling. Luckily I have a sweet friend who invited me out with her family to dinner, and it ended up being a great time. But what had me thinking and a bit concerned is that I would probably feel like that way more often if I allowed myself not to have plans every once in awhile. Sometimes it is good to fight those feelings and force yourself to be strong and bear a lonely Friday night. But then other times you do need friends and to not be alone. When I am feeling that way, I tend to get even sadder about being single. I notice my singleness way more and get frustrated because all I want is a man to spend my Friday nights with where it isn't even a question whether I will be alone or not. But until then, I am learning and growing to be comfortable in my discomfort.

The Dreaded Events as a Single

As we progress in life and more and more people get married, there are many more weddings to attend or be a part of. It gets harder and harder going to such events as a single person because it seems like everyone else is dating someone or already married. I was even in a wedding where a guy I dated, which was not a good situation, was now dating my friend, and all three of us were in the wedding together. Talk about a challenge! I had to muster up all the courage and joy I possibly could in order to tough it out through the wedding. I definitely had fun, but it was just the stigma of it all that had me down at times. I know if I had heard of someone in my situation, I would have felt for them. Not only are weddings all around, but there are BBQs, birthday parties, and the dreaded high school reunion that no one wants to show up to single. I remember I used to think that I better have a boyfriend by then. And here I am, six months from my high school reunion, and no potential relationship in sight. It is hard to see how it will happen or if it will even happen.

And if I am still single by my high school reunion, again I will need to muster up all the confidence and dignity I have within me and hold my head high once more. I have done it before, and I can do it again. But honestly I don't want to have to do that. I want to go with a man I love who I see a future with. I want to tell of our beautiful love story. I want people to be happy for me and not pity me. I think that is what makes it so much worse is that people actually pity you. As if being single is the absolute worst thing that could ever happen. I guess that is one of the many reasons I am writing this book. I want to break these preconceived ideas that singleness is like a cancer, and it cannot be cured until you are no longer single. It is nothing of the sort, even though it is hard and lonely at times.

But it can also be so beautiful. It can be inspiring to others depending on how you use your single season. There are different seasons of life, and none are better than the other but each one is very different. So let's stop comparing where we are at. Let's enjoy these seasons and events in between, where others might expect us to be depressed and pathetic, yet we are fulfilled, happy and content as a single person. We are doing the impossible!

And can I give you an update about my high school reunion. As I write, it is now past my ten-year reunion, and I did the impossible. I attended it, single as can be, and had a great time! I felt more myself, more confident and more secure than I ever have. It did not bother me about being there single, and no one even said much about my relationship status. If anything, I made jokes about it because that is just my personality. I think it is funny a lot of times that I am still single and have not been in a committed relationship yet. It doesn't make sense to me and won't until I meet my future husband, so for now I laugh about it. We can't take life and ourselves too seriously because life is what it is and we can't control it. We just have to go with the flow and enjoy ourselves to the best of our ability.

Friendships Change

Lately, I am noticing my friendships have changed a lot with my girlfriends. I did just move back from living in Australia for two years, so obviously things have changed. I have changed and so have they. But what I am finding so hard is finding someone to talk about my singleness with. Most of my good friends are married or dating, so I automatically feel weird talking to them about it. It seems like they don't really know what to say when I do happen to bring it up. I honestly think they feel bad for me and don't know how to comfort me in it because they are now happily out of that season. But then I even have a couple single girlfriends, and I find we just aren't on the same page with being single. They are up for dating around and having fun. Now there is nothing wrong with that; it's just I'm not in that place at this point. I am serious about finding someone I want to spend the rest of my life with.

In Australia, I had so many single friends. The majority of my friends were single, so to come home and there be such a drastic shift is more challenging than I thought it would be. I find myself feeling more out of place, and then it makes me sad that I still haven't met someone yet. And I forgot how married couples, at least my friends who have been married less than five years, always want to be together. I remember the days of girls' nights happening more often than not. But it seems like that won't be happening very much anymore. And I am sure I would not mind that if I too were married or in a relationship. But when men are around, you don't have the same kind of conversations. There is a lot less girl talk, and I miss that.

I didn't really anticipate it being like this, and it makes being single so much harder. When you don't have girlfriends on the same page as you to encourage each other and pray with one another, it makes singleness very lonely. I am sure with time things will get better in this area. I may need to get bold and talk to my girlfriends about it anyway even if they don't understand. But they should understand because they were once single too even if it wasn't for as long as I have been. When I do finally meet my man and am in a relationship, I want to make sure I am still there for people who are single. It is so important to remember these times in our life and how we feel, so that later on we can help and encourage someone else.

What I can do now is pray that God brings some single girls into my life that are on the same page. Other women who aren't complaining about it all the time, but who are on the journey and moving forward in fullness. It helps to process and learn together how to make the most out of your singleness. It creates accountability and a support system. It is also important to keep your friendships with your married and dating friends even if it has changed and is different. You can learn from all stages of your friends' lives, single or not.

21.

I Can't Do This Anymore

Have you ever felt like you just can't do it anymore? You can't go through another glimmer of hope in regards to a potential relationship all to find it is snuffed out by yet another disappointment? I am so over waiting at this point. I have been so hopeful and excited about the future, and then, another guy once again disappoints me. And to top it off, I start to think back to all my other misfortunes when it comes to guys that didn't work out and see how happy they are in their new relationships. And here I am...still single. How does it happen? How does the guy get away with breaking my heart and then gets to move onto someone else and is happy as can be? It isn't fair.

But what I have learned is life isn't fair and that includes love. It isn't fair who we are attracted to or who we fall for. Sometimes we fall for the wrong ones. Sometimes we try to make it work with someone it was never meant to work with. Sometimes we fall way too many times and struggle to get back up again. But as long as we keep on going, despite how we may feel, despite how hurt we have been. I have been feeling the downside of singleness lately. But God reassures me through his word in Joel 2:25-26 (NIV),

"I will repay you for the years the locusts have eaten—
the great locust and the young locust,
the other locusts and the locust swarm—
my great army that I sent among you.
You will have plenty to eat, until you are full,
and you will praise the name of the Lord your God,
who has worked wonders for you;
never again will my people be shamed."

I don't know about you, but I have had a lot of locusts eat away at my life in the past. I have had heartbreak after heartbreak, loss after loss, and I won't take it anymore. God promises to make beauty out of ashes and that He will give us fullness and wonder, and we will never be shamed again. I believe this relates to our years of singleness as well, where we have felt difficulty and defeat. Where we have seen our dreams slip away from us. But any dream that has gone and left us has not been fulfilled yet because God has a bigger and better dream. The guy you thought you were going to marry is nothing compared to the man God has for you. We must remember the dreams He has placed in our hearts and not shy away; but we must declare them and believe God will bring them to pass in the most exciting of ways. It will be better than we could have ever imagined!

The Desire

Sometimes the desire to be in a relationship and get married is so strong it is annoying. I think what annoys me more is that when people are in a relationship or are engaged, they are much happier.

My goal in singleness has been to be happy regardless of my circumstances - of whether I have a guy interested in me or not, whether I am dating someone or not. Although it is true that we will be happy when we meet the man of our dreams, it doesn't mean we can't be happy now. But I think we will experience a different kind of happiness, and that is okay because it is something to look forward to. But our future happiness doesn't mean it has to steal from our happiness now.

What makes you happy? There is so much to make you happy now in this season of life. There is so much joy to experience; there are so many things you can do in this season that you won't be able to do once you are in a relationship and especially once you get married. Do the things you love and live your dreams now. Time doesn't stand still in singleness, though it can feel like it. It feels like we are at a standstill, while everyone passes us by with engagements, weddings and babies. But we are in a different time zone. We have more alone time than those passing us by, so what can we do now that we can't once we are married?

Many times I have wished that I could just lose the desire to be in a relationship and married altogether. It would be easier. I have lived this long without anyone, and I am sure I could keep on living on my own happily single. But then there is this gnawing feeling and desire to find the love of my life, and it won't go away as much as I have tried. I have tried convincing myself, that I don't need to be in a relationship, which I don't, but I want to be. I have tried convincing myself that I want to be single, but the truth is I don't. I have been single for long enough, and I want to be in a relationship that leads to marriage. And that is okay if that is what I want. What's hard is I know what I want, but a lot of guys don't. Once a guy knows what he wants, he goes for it; a real man does anyway. And that is what I am looking for, a real man who has the same desires and isn't afraid to show it. So why hasn't it happened yet?

I do not know the answer to that question, but what I do know is that for where my life has taken me so far, I am glad I wasn't in a relationship. I was able to move to Sydney, Australia for two years and fully dedicate my life to God and what He wanted to do in me. Yes, of course I was hoping I would meet someone while I was there and have memories from there together. But looking back, I praise God I didn't meet someone there. Those two years are what really helped me grow into my singleness and more importantly in my relationship with God. He was my sole provider in every sense. I had no one else or nothing, but Him to see me through.

The desire is still there. And it will be there until I get married and a new desire will form, probably for children. This is the way life works and rather than fighting it, I accept it and learn from it. I don't let it stifle me or cause me pain, but I choose to let it excite me and change me. I choose to let it stir passion within me and grow my love, so when it is time for it to come to pass, I will be full and ready to give to someone the love God intended for them and me. I encourage you to do the same.

Contentment

I am content in my singleness. I never thought I would be. I thought I would always desperately long for someone in my life that would take care of me and fill the voids I once had. But I have experienced something so much better than that. I now have a wholeness that has been filled by the Holy Spirit where I no longer look to another person to make me happy. I am content in myself because of my relationship with God. I may not love my life circumstances at the moment, but I am able to find the joy in it. I am able to be thankful for this funny transition season I am in. It may not look the way I thought my life would by this age. But when is life ever what you thought it would be? And somehow it shows itself to be even better than we expected in its own funny way.

This contentment I have found was through no means of my own. But it was through Jesus Christ. It sounds crazy to me that this is even possible because the way I used to feel was so the opposite of how I feel now. I knew it was possible for God to change my life, but I never realized it could be this good. I struggled for so long with my self-worth and value and always looked to guys to fulfill that in me. It only ever made it worse, but my despair would take over making it so hard to see my future and what was ahead of me. I always believed contentment and goodwill for others, but I found it hard to see it for myself. But God has made me more than content with myself. He has helped me love myself. Old insecurities no longer weigh me down. Old thinking has no place in my life anymore. Anytime one of those old thoughts of not feeling good enough creep in, I stand on the words He has gently spoken to me, and I hold onto them.

Honestly I don't know how people go through life without Jesus guiding them, speaking to them, and loving on them. He is always trying to do those things with us; He tried with me for years. But until I chose Him back and decided to follow Him, listen to Him, and love Him, I was constantly in turmoil searching for something I could not find. Always looking for something to define me and tell me who I was, only made the wrong people tell me lies about myself, making it even harder to find what I was searching for. But God saw me all along. He was just waiting for me to look up at Him, so He could give me what I really needed and not what I thought I needed.

Contentment is not happiness or joy, but it is an assurance in who you are and whose you are. It is a stance in life where you do not let emotions and circumstances sway you in any way. It is a place of peace and not of settling. Contentment does not mean you settle for where you are at in life, and you lose the desire for more out of life. But contentment serves as a peace that surpasses all understanding. Others may look at you and think *why is she doing so well when her life looks like this or that? Or how can she be so content when her life isn't going the way she wanted it?* Our culture tends to dictate what our lives should look like rather than what they are intended to look like. There is a difference. God never thinks we should be anything we aren't already. He never thinks we should be doing this job, or have this car, or be in that relationship. Those are people's opinions. God intends good things for us. But *good* to Him oftentimes looks much different than what the world thinks. He doesn't care much about how well you are doing with your sales at work as long as you are trying. God cares about all the details of our lives, but He isn't interested in how well you are doing externally and how people perceive your life. He cares about your heart and whether you are growing in Him. Is your relationship with Him close and strong? He wants to be in every step you take. Not because He is controlling but because He wants to take care of you. He wants to help you. True contentment is when you live how you were intended to live...with Him every step of the way, listening, and loving Him.

22.

Trust God in the Process

I love how we can trust God with our lives and major decisions, but we can't trust him to bring our husbands to us. We think we need to make something happen, and too often than not, we fall on our faces in the process. We think we know better. We think we know what we want only to find out how wrong we really are. As women we have a natural tendency to manipulate situations to get what we want. We obsess and process about how we can possibly make something happen with the cute guy down the hall or the guy at the coffee shop we see every morning. We tend to think God doesn't have it all sorted and planned out, and ultimately deep down we think we can do better, at least that is what we are telling Him by not trusting.

What trusting looks like is not worrying. How good are we as women at worrying. If we aren't worried, we start worrying that we aren't worried. We stress ourselves out over things we have no control over. We believe that if we aren't worried, then it won't get done. But trusting God and not worrying looks like being confident in the promise God has given you for getting married. It looks like you going after big dreams and goals and not allowing your singleness to dictate what you do in life. It looks like you being excited for your future regardless of any prospects of a husband in front of you.

Trusting God with this season of your life will be what sets up your marriage and your future family. If you can learn to trust God now, not only will your single season flourish personally, but also it will set the foundation for your marriage. You can only go up from here. God has the best for you, and in order to have the best, you must believe in the best. There is more for you than you even know. He is changing you from the inside out, and it is hard work, but so worth it when you see all He has done in you.

Every time you sense or feel yourself starting to worry or wonder when the guy is going to ask you out, or when the sparks will fly with a stranger, remind yourself that God's got it. And if that guy you have your eye on is the one for you, then it will happen. So often I get frustrated as to why a guy I may find attractive or I am interested in doesn't pursue me when he clearly seems interested, but I always have to tell myself that if he isn't my husband than I am not interested anyway. And if he is my husband, then God will make it happen eventually. All I can do is keep praying, holding onto my convictions, believing for the best, and know that when the time is right, it will happen. Actually doing that and letting go and giving it to God is a hard pill to swallow. But each time you do it, it gets easier and easier and that much closer to your dream coming true.

Character is Key

Character is the foundation on which we build our lives and make decisions off of. Not only is your character key, but the character of the man you are hoping to marry is key as well. You can tell a person's character by what they say and do. Does what they say translate into what they do and vice versa? I challenge you, as well, to consider your words and actions. The wilderness of singleness is a time to sort out your character. It is a time to grow and be strengthened in the character flaws you may possess. Be the person you hope to marry. If you wouldn't want to date or marry who you are right now, then maybe you need more time to become that person. You don't need to feel condemned about this or bad about yourself. We all need time to grow in certain areas before we are ready to enter into a lasting relationship. It is for your future family's benefit that you do not rush into anything and that you choose the harder road sometimes to face the uncomfortable and grow into who you are.

Once you have a pretty good foundation, you will have a better view when choosing the right person for you. Sometimes we tend to be attracted to the wrong men because we do not see their true character. The way to see someone's true character is through time and boundaries. When you place healthy boundaries where they need to be, you will be able to see if someone will respect those or not. If they cannot respect boundaries, they do not respect you and are a waste of your time. You may think that they will learn this over time, but believe me, if they do not respect you from the start, they won't ten years down the road.

Character is a serious thing to look at when potentially dating someone. People are who they are because of the character they have allowed to be built in their lives or the lack of. Everyone faces struggles, and it is how they deal with these that determine who a person will be. Another good way to indicate someone's character is to see how they treat others. Many times guys will put on a good face in order to woo and charm you, until you find out later it was all just an act to reel you in. It is upsetting to think someone would do that, but it happens all the time. Even more disappointing is when the show goes on so long it leads to marriage, only to find out after who he really is. This isn't meant to scare you, but to bring awareness to the reality that is out there. You may have already experienced someone like this.

It is heartbreaking and hard to understand that someone would deceive you. But the good news is we can catch it early on through discernment of the Holy Spirit. He will guide us as we listen closely and stay alert. We have nothing to fear or worry about when we are close to the Father who is there to protect us.

Bold Love

Don't be afraid to love. Don't be afraid to put yourself out there with family and friends. Once you can do that, you can be fierce in your love with your future husband. I know that hurt takes us out sometimes, and it can take us awhile to get back up and try again. But when you are ready, go back at it again. Bold love looks like loving without expectation of getting anything in return. It is letting the love of your Heavenly Father overflow onto others. When we know how much God loves us and are filled with His love, we can give that love freely to others.

I know sometimes this is easier said than done like most things in life. But loving boldly and without reservation is the most freeing thing you can do. Not only are you helping yourself, but you are helping others when you give of love unsparingly. Sometimes we go through seasons when this actually isn't possible for us to do because maybe we are recovering after too many heartbreaks that left us with nothing else to give. I have been there. When you feel this emptiness inside, and all you want is to get back the love you once had for others and for life; but all that is left is a few broken pieces of a heart that once felt so full and big.

But there is good news for us when we hit these seasons. God does not let us stay there in the brokenness we feel. He gently and sweetly looks after those broken pieces and slowly starts to mend them back together better than they were before they were ever shattered. He patiently waits for us to hand over to Him each piece that was left on the floor. He reaches out to us and looks at us with the loving eyes of a Heavenly Father, adoringly. He reassures us that He is not going to break it more, but He is going to mend it as painlessly as possible with few stitches like the work of the best heart surgeon there is. And once He masterfully sews it back together, He checks our vitals to make sure that everything is working, as it should.

Once he sees that we are able to breathe a bit easier, He lifts our chin to lock eyes and reassures us that everything is going to be okay, and with each day we will gain strength with our new heart. Eventually we will not feel so tired and overwhelmed. As time goes by, it will get easier and easier to slowly but surely love again. But not just love in a superficial way, or a "because we-have-to" kind of way, but in a bold and confident love that could only be a product of the love He has for us.

This kind of love is self-sacrificing, humbling, challenging, relentless, and unwavering. It is not based on feelings, but it is based on action. It is speaking life into others and letting the Holy Spirit speak through you. It is encouraging people even when it may be uncomfortable for you. Bold love does not need love in return because it knows who its source is.

I have gone through seasons of having bold love and others where I have not. I have used bold love on the wrong people, in the wrong circumstances. But what I have learned is that even if it is used wrongly, God will heal and mend and help us try again in the right way. So I do not have to worry or be upset when I am going through a season of receiving love rather than giving it. I try my best, no matter which season, but ultimately when the time has come - Jesus will revive this love again and help me give it out where it is needed. The ultimate commandment from God is to love Him and love people. If we give Him our best efforts, He will meet us where we are at and show us how to love all over again.

Fulfilled

I find myself in a place I never thought I would get to. I am fulfilled. For all of my life I had been looking to the future thinking that what I had in front of me was never good enough. I constantly wished and hoped for a boyfriend thinking that would make me happy. I thought having a man love me and me love him would be the ultimate reality. And of course I still cannot wait for that day. But recently I have been asked multiple times if I am dating someone. Even men have been asking me. They mean it in the best sense. They assume I have someone in my life because I am so happy and fulfilled right now. I am more confident than ever, and I never thought I could get here...single.

This has been one of my biggest goals in my single season. I have wanted to be fulfilled and whole without anyone else in my life besides Jesus of course. That is what is so great about it all. I have found Him more present in my life because I am more focused on Him rather than focused on other men. I honestly never thought this would be possible. I am not saying my desire for a husband has left me, but I am surer than ever that God will bring him into my life when the time is right.

I am not sure where you find yourself on the journey of being happy in your singleness. I am not sure if you are on a mountaintop and happy in your singleness or if you are in one of the pits and valleys of the journey where it is hard to see what is in the distant near future. But I want you to know that you can and will get through it, and God will show you things in this time of wilderness that you never thought He could. Some things that have helped me find this sense of fulfillment have been being obedient to God, first and foremost. To live life with an expectation that there is something right-around-the-corner for you whether that is today, tomorrow or years from now. I encourage you to find joy in the little things of life. Go to a cute cafe and have a coffee with yourself. Plan dates for yourself, by yourself or with girlfriends.

Don't waste time moping around and be present when you do those things.

Too often I have made the mistake of wishing I was with my future husband experiencing some of the things I have. And of course, that is so real. But there is a fine line in wishing and wallowing. The Bible tells us we already have all that we need, and it is hard to believe sometimes, especially when you may be in a financial lack or circumstances aren't in your favor, but it really is true. Internally when we have the Holy Spirit within us, we do not lack. Outwardly things may not be ideal, but we have been created and equipped to take on these circumstances and stand in the peace God has already given us.

Fulfillment looks different for everyone. Yours may look different than mine. But I challenge you to start finding what that looks like for you in your single season, and it will then stay with you beyond this season and into every other season as well. What is your go-to? What makes you happy and content? What brings you joy? Sometimes those are some of the hardest questions to answer, especially in a tough season. But wrestle with God on these things. He will reveal the answers to you if you do not already know. And start doing what you love the best way you can and watch the blessings and fulfillment pour through. When you are happy and content, blessings seem to follow you wherever you go, no matter what happens.

Prayer is Powerful

Praying and thanking God in advance is one of the best things you can do while in your season of waiting. This is not just for singleness, but in all waiting seasons. But I especially want to cover prayer during your time of being single. As you wait for your *Prince Charming* to be awakened, you don't know what he is facing in life at this very moment, so start praying for him now. Don't just pray for him to come into your life, but pray for him where he is at, no matter how long it takes for you to meet him. He may be in an unhealthy relationship that he needs to be done with or facing a parent's death or in between jobs and losing confidence within himself. Whatever it is, you can start praying for him now, and God will lead you in what to pray if you are unsure.

Prayer is a powerful weapon that we can use to fight off the enemy and his nonsense. God has given us the gift of prayer so that we would use it, and this season of waiting is the perfect time to get on our knees and pray unceasingly. It isn't just so that we can make things happen that we want to, but it is to protect and guard their future and yours together. It isn't to prevent things from happening or to speed things up; it is to stand in the gap for your future family and get a head start for what is ahead.

Not only am I praying for my future husband, but I have started a journal where I write to him which I mentioned before. I want him to know where I am at while I wait for him. It also helps me understand that he is real and that he does exist. Even if it is just for that, to help you realize that he is somewhere in the world and he will come into your life at the right time, is encouraging. We have all seen things like this done before, and I always think about how cute it would be to give your husband something like that when you meet him. But actually doing it, it is not so cute. It feels awkward and weird while I write my heart out to a man that does not exist in my life yet.

But this is the way in which God works. He puts a dream in our heart, and while we wait for it and sit on it, we need to put some action to it for it to come to pass. And these are my action steps. There are also things you can do to honor your husband now like when I have taken six months to not date but instead dedicated time to God and specifically for my husband. We must sacrifice things in relationships so why not start now. It doesn't have to be no dating at all until you meet him because how will you meet him if you aren't willing to go on a date with him. But God will prompt you with these steps to take in different seasons and you can obey them and take them on or not. No one is forcing you, but I do believe it helps. It helps keep you focused on what you do want and helps you get stronger and more confident in who you are during your single season.

Someone recently challenged me to start praying strategic prayers. Pray specific prayers that will help guide you in choosing the right man for you. Pray for peace when you meet him. Pray that he would have the same values as you when it comes to your relationship with God and if church is a priority for you that it would be for him as well. Now I don't recommend praying that he has blonde hair and blue eyes or that he is 6 ft 4 inches because as soon as you meet someone like that you may think he is the one and when he definitely is not. And God has a funny sense of humor if you haven't already found that out. I find that many married couples actually had always-preferred looks opposite to what their now husband or wife looks like. But they still find them to be the most attractive person they have ever seen. God tends to change our hearts on things that we once thought we would never like or do and low and behold it happens. And obviously we all know it shouldn't be about looks anyway right? But it does help. You definitely need to be attracted to your future husband and you will be. God wouldn't do that to you.

Pray also that he would come into your life. There is nothing wrong with praying him into your next season. I used to think that I couldn't do that because I have in the past and he never showed up. But if your heart is in the right place and you are wanting to get married for the right reasons then by all means, pray for him to come into your life. God is not withholding him because He is mean and doesn't want you to have him. He wants more than anything to bring your husband into your life. He is just waiting for the both of you to be ready. So keep praying for him and for you. And trust that God has it covered.

Singleness is not a journey to do alone so pray with other girlfriends who are either on the same journey or even ones who are already married. Praying with another person can be even more powerful at times and they can speak things that you cannot yet voice for yourself. Sometimes we can be too afraid to pray the things we really want to, and praying with another person, God can speak those things through them, which can be even more profound for you.

Praying is also very powerful when dating someone. As humans we want to control things, and especially as women we like to know what is going on at all times. But so often we end up leading conversations in a relationship where we should actually be letting the man take the lead. For instance, when dating someone and wondering your status of the relationship, often times we want to know before the guy is ready to even talk about it. This causes strife and frustration for both you and him. The best thing to do is pray that God would make those important conversations happen. When we do this, more often than not the man is the one to bring those topics up and lead it. And if he doesn't and you are still waiting around months longer than you would have liked to wait, he might not be the one for you. If a relationship is causing you anxiety and stress more often than not, it may not be the right person for you. In every season of your singleness be prayerful and watch what God will do.

23.

Strong and Single

I am a strong woman. I know what I want, and I don't apologize for it. I'm not harsh or mean, but I can be pretty direct depending on the situation. I have big dreams and goals. I work hard, and I am not afraid to step out and succeed. This was not always my case, but God has really shown me how to be a strong woman in the best sense. He has shown me that strong does not have to be confrontational. Strong is not inflexible, but strong is adaptable. I love being a strong woman, and I surround myself with other strong women; and I encourage such qualities.

But what I have found is that it is hard being a strong woman when it comes to dating. Men are intimidated by strength, not all men. But if they have any ounce of insecurity ruling them, then they will run from such women. They may be intrigued at first, but over time I think they get scared and run off. They usually run off into the arms of a less strong woman, a woman who may be struggling with her own insecurity as well. It is safer when you aren't with someone who is committed to being challenged and challenging. It is work to grow and become strong. It takes a lot of time and effort, and sometimes people do not want to make the sacrifice.

What makes it worse is that strong women easily fall for the wrong guys. We have trouble finding men who are just as strong as us, and we tend to be the ones who end up more like caregivers if we are not careful. Unfortunately these wrong guys don't see what is happening. Or they do, and they take advantage until they are ready to move on and be with someone who won't push them to confront what they need to take on.

There is also the other side of being a strong woman where no one is ever good enough for you. You keep men at a distance because you think you can do things on your own better than if you were with someone. You don't want anyone cramping your style so you stay in your single bubble, all the while complaining about being single. Men can sense your self-reliance, and it is like repellant to them because they want a woman who may not need them but does want them around and a woman who will ask for help just because he can help.

All of this to say, it is hard. But it is worth it. Because you are strong, you will eventually attract a strong man, key word being man, who will understand your lioness tendencies and better yet, he will appreciate them. Maybe you don't consider yourself this type of woman, but let me encourage you that you are. Every woman has it in her to be strong, bold and still beautiful. It took me awhile to consider myself strong and bold. It was a journey I had to go on, one filled with some face plants and insecurities pouring out of me. But I am so glad I committed to it, and I continue to. It is a life-long journey; where you will face difficulties that will tempt you to shrink back or you can rise up. It is your choice.

Rise up

I believe God is rising up strong, single women who know what they want and where they are going. Gone are the days of uncertain women who follow the crowd. Women have been put down, beaten and battered for too long. Our King is bringing his royal daughters to the forefront of an Esther-like time in history where "such a time as this." Women are done with men treating them like they are an object to be owned or had. God's kingdom will prevail and women have been the missing piece of a beautiful story of strength and dignity.

He has fashioned them to be a force to be reckoned with through their femininity. God has a way of bringing women together better than men could ever do. A band of women are rising up, coming together, and using their voice to yell loudly to the rest of the world that enough is enough. Long-gone are the days of oppression that have kept women in bondage for centuries. Gone are the days when women let insecurity rule them, but now their God-given authority reigns amongst the darkness that has tried to take the hearts of men. The darkness has tried to seep into the awestruck wonder of a King who never created men and women to act this way. He is calling both men and women to join forces and defend those who cannot defend themselves. He is reaching out and seeing who will reach back to live a life that is worth His glory and goodness.

The good news is that there are women who are ready to join the battle and fight for what is right. There are women who are fed up with believing the lies the world has offered to them since they were a child. The lies that tell you: you aren't good enough, worthy enough, beautiful enough, strong enough. The enemy has tried to keep us down and in the shadows. But the Savior of the world is about to unleash a new kind of woman, one who is no longer afraid of the world seeing who she truly is...whole, confident and bold. The enemy is so scared for what is about to come out of the bride of Christ. She is no longer something to marvel at or be confused by. She now knows her purpose and is ready to go for what has been stirring in her heart all of these years.

But it all begins with the one. And ladies, it is our responsibility to move things forward and not let our baggage and bondage keep us weighed down and dragging our chains. Release yourselves into the unknown and watch what your groom does with your willingness and heart.

Confident to the Core

Confidence is something we all want and need. Confidence helps us overcome our fears and insecurities. It helps us feel strong and powerful in our own skin. It gives us the extra oomph we need to succeed. With confidence we can achieve anything we put our minds to. But so often we think confidence is something we find within ourselves. We think that if we can lose those extra few pounds, we will feel more confident in our bodies. Or that confidence comes from another person, and once we find someone to love us, then we will feel confident. But there is a different kind of confidence that will take us much further than any of those things.

If we are going to live a life full of freedom and the way God intended us to live, we need confidence from Him. We need Him to show us who we are so that we can feel satisfied in ourselves and in our lives. Without this godly confidence, we will not only struggle in relationships, but we will struggle in all areas of our lives. The enemy's goal for us is that we lose confidence or never find it, so we can stay confined to where we are rather than growing into our potential to accomplish all that is set out for us.

Even once we are in a relationship, our confidence will be tested. Bringing another person along for the ride in your personal journey will only highlight the things you do not like about yourself. This is when it will become a temptation to focus on all those things and let them eat away at you until there is nothing left to be confident in. We say we want a relationship, but once we do find a great guy, it is still going to take some effort to push through some insecurity that will surface through the process.

Confidence can be hard depending on your life circumstances and experiences. For some they have not had anyone to encourage and lift them up. Even worse some people have been torn down their whole lives. I grew up in an unstable environment that made it hard to be sure of anything or anyone, especially myself. So it was quite the expedition of growing and moving past the roadblocks and barricades that had formed within my life. It took a whole lot of gumption and strength to break through these barriers. It wasn't easy; it was painful and took a lot longer than I would have wanted. But the more I fought for myself and the self worth that I so lacked early on in life, the more I gained. It was a battle that I lost more often than not. It took me falling on my face a few times, but each one of those failures and mistakes along the way brought me to where I am today.

I am now victorious and more confident than ever. I am not confident in my own abilities because that is much scarier. I am confident in who God has created me to be, confident in the gifts He has given me, confident in what I am called to, and the rest is history. I know the battle isn't completely over. I am sure in the future, single or married, I will face more fights with insecurities and doubts. But with God leading me, I have nothing to fear. He will help me move past it and gain more confidence than I even have now.

Intimidating

Have you ever been told that you are intimidating by a guy? Has it made you feel upset and mad at yourself as if there is something wrong with you? I know I can be intimidating to guys. I have been told so, and I have seen it. I used to want to change that about myself and figured it was a wall I was putting up, trying to keep guys away from me. What I have realized is that I did build a wall, and it is one that keeps all the boys away - but the men will stay. I saw a t-shirt today that says, "Strong women intimidate boys...and excite men." And it is so true. Your strength, when you let it shine through, will scare all the boys away. But you don't want a boy at the end of the day anyway. Sure, boys are fun to play with, but we aren't in grade school anymore. We want men to be excited by us and to excite us through adventure and challenge. It is what we are made for. So be confident in your strength as a woman. Don't shy away from speaking up or being who you are because there are a bunch of boys around. Your intimidation is protection from all the wrong kinds. It doesn't have to be a negative thing. Real men love a challenge and aren't afraid of a strong woman. So let's rise up and be who we are called to be, and don't apologize for it.

Strong men need a strong woman. It won't work otherwise because there will be one more powerful than the other. We may be called to submit, but submission takes strength as well when you are already a strong woman. It goes both ways, men can be intimidating. But you don't need to be intimidated by someone else and the way they may be or appear to be. Be confident in you, and the courage will come.

Take it as a compliment that you are intimidating. You scare boys; men may be scared, but they won't let fear get in the way. Boys are too afraid to go for what they want and resort to less scary options. Boys don't like to be challenged. They want to be babied and cared for. I don't know about you, but I don't want a full-grown adult acting like a baby. I want a man who can take care of himself, but who will let me care for him. Caring for and taking care of are two very different things.

24.

One Day...

We have all made statements like, "One day when...I..." And sometimes there is nothing wrong with saying such things. But something I have learned along my single life is that if my "one day when's" outweigh me actually doing things, that's when I need to change. I used to hold off experiencing some things in life thinking that I wanted to do them with a boyfriend or my future husband. And yes, I still have some of those bucket list things such as going to Bora Bora for my honeymoon. Obviously I can't go on a honeymoon by myself. But there are other things that I think so often we have a dream of doing, and we keep putting it off because we are afraid to do it alone or we are afraid we will miss out on other things. But what you are truly missing out on is experiencing something of a lifetime that can grow you and change you for the better.

Life is too short to sit around waiting for a guy to come into your life so life can happen. Life doesn't happen to you, it happens through you. And without you being purposeful and pursuing the things God has placed on your heart, then it can't happen. Why waste time waiting on your future husband when you could have some of the best memories of your life in your singlehood, and you will get to share with him everything you did when the time is right. And you never know you could meet him in the midst of doing one of your bucket list experiences. *One day* mentalities are for people who have their head in the clouds, but who aren't willing to ever hit the ground running and actually get it done.

Dreaming and scheming is fun and romantic. But it is just like marriage, it may look romantic and beautiful on the outside, but it is a lot of work once you're on the inside. But that is what makes it beautiful and worth it. Just like the waiting season of singleness, that is what makes the actual meeting of your future husband and your story together so beautiful. It just isn't very beautiful at first when you are right in the middle of it waiting for it to go somewhere and take off. But I believe when you have really committed yourself to making the best out of your days of singleness that is when an ease and flow comes into the beginning stages of your relationship. Your 'one day' will be worth it when you make the most out of your everyday.

Dream into Reality

Here I am, sitting in a beautiful little mountain home surrounded by trees, sitting by a fireplace with a dog at my feet. My favorite old classics, Etta James Pandora is playing. I'm drinking coffee and sitting on a comfy leather couch. I am living one of my dream weekends, yet I find myself a little lonely and bored to be honest. I always think this is what I want, to be alone with no distractions. Yet I find distractions anyway. I am dedicating this weekend to writing this book, and I am tired. I just want to watch a movie and fall asleep. I can't help but think how much better this weekend would be with the love of my life sitting next to me quietly reading. Just his presence would make me more comfortable. But here I am, alone, with no one but the dog to talk to.

This is the life of a single girl. The struggle with wanting to be independent and the desire to have a man you can depend on. I always romanticize ideas in my head thinking how great it would be, and then I find myself in this place of "okay...now what." I get bored of writing at times; it's a discipline, and sometimes I just don't want to do it. But isn't that the case with most things in life. As a single girl (my whole life), I have dreamed of the day when I will be married and everything will be rosy and beautiful. But just with how I have thought up my little writer's retreat, the same goes for most other things in life like a wedding day. For me, what I have imagined in my head is always better than reality. It is important to have high expectations while relishing in the realities we are living in. For instance, I could easily be let down with the way my weekend is turning out. Or I could take it all in and focus on the unexpected beauty. As I look around and really think about this opportunity I have been given, I am grateful. Time alone is good for the soul, and I will wish I had these days back once I am elbow deep in diapers and kid's toys. We must continue to dream, but also let our reality surprise us.

I'm sure that in the future I will have a weekend like this one again, but with my husband sitting next to me. We will be able to take breaks from our reading, writing or whatever else we are doing and go for a hike or just laugh and cuddle. My life will not always consist of being single and always having to have these beautiful experiences alone. But how thankful I am, for these times alone determine how much I will appreciate my husband when he is here with me. How we live our single life is a reflection of how we will live our married one.

I am determined to live life to the fullest, the best way I can, on my own because it will make life with someone else that much sweeter. I want to keep raising the invisible bar in my own life because we only have one shot at this, and I want to live it exceptionally. I want to be inspired and encouraged by the beauty and people around me. I sit here, alone, and working on a project (this book) in hopes that it will challenge, inspire, and comfort my fellow single girls to live, not sitting around and waiting, but LIVE your life holding nothing back. I believe I will have many more experiences like the one I am sitting in where I will stop, recognize, and appreciate the once in a lifetime experience that it is. When I look at it that way, my spirit is lifted, and I am ready to squeeze all the potential that this weekend holds.

Don't Sell Yourself Short

For some odd reason, for years women have settled. They have settled for mediocre in the men they choose. They settle for living in the shadows of a man because they think that is what submission is. They quiet their voice to the point they don't even realize they have one anymore. They think if they are too pro-women they are annoying feminist who will never get married. We live under our potential because we are afraid of all we are truly capable of.

So why do we do it to ourselves? Why are we hiding from what God wants to do in and through our lives? We cripple ourselves with fear that is just as unrealistic as our high hopes and dreams. I'm not sure about you, but I would rather choose to believe in the unrealistic goals I have then the ridiculous lies that I have believed for way too long. There is way too much for us to do and change in the world, then we are allowing ourselves -and all for what purpose? Men at times don't respect us either way, whether we hide and shy away or when we rise above and stand out. So you choose which way you want to go and how you want to be known. I would much rather be intimidating than a doormat.

If we don't believe in ourselves, no one else will. Until we can say *this is who I am, what I am about and where I am going* - then no one else can or will see it. Or they will try to tell you who you are not, which will only lead to you knowing less of your true potential. I used to hate the word *potential* because to me it meant I was far off, but potential is not where you aren't, but it is where you are going! Potential is what gives you a foundation to build upon and take off on. Without potential, you are at ground zero with no tools or skills to build with. I have now come to terms with the word potential, and I hope I never stop having it.

When others try to tear you down, don't let them. Men have this tendency to do so when they themselves feel inadequate and threatened. They look to you for their security and when you can't fulfill that need in their lives, they move on to the next girl who might have the "magic touch" all to find themselves with years wasted with a woman who leaves them empty and bored because there was no challenge in any of the relationship. No matter who you are, you need to be challenged. Challenge is what grows you and makes life interesting. Some men want it easy and uneventful, comfortable, smooth sailing. But you are not a woman who wants a man like that. You wouldn't be reading this book if you wanted a man like that. No, you want a man who will push you and bring you to a place where you never thought you could reach. You want a man who makes you focus and feel confident to take on whatever the world throws at you and whatever dreams and goals you want to accomplish. You want a man who isn't ashamed to be behind you and support you in your pursuit of your calling. But that is because you are a woman who will do the same for him. So let those other boys go, the ones who don't see you for who you really are. They aren't worth a minute of your time, and frankly, they don't deserve it either.

They have more growing up to do, and you are already on your way. Do not let someone hold you back. As soon as you sense someone is holding you back or not letting you be free in who you are, it may be time to reevaluate that friendship or relationship, whether they are male or female. We have things to do and places to go, and if you are allowing someone to rule you then see what needs to be changed and make it happen.

25.

Putting My Dreams Aside

When I was in my early twenties and even in high school, I used to dream of the day I would have a family of my own. It was the only thing that got me through some of the hard times. God had put this insatiable desire in me for a family of my own where I could rewrite history and the years of generational hurt and destruction that had plagued my childhood and adolescence. I dreamed of having a good marriage full of love and respect for one another where we would never fight in front of our children, where we would never bring them into our problems, but we would constantly build them up and encourage them. I dreamed of a peaceful home where the kids could bring their friends to and not ever feel like they have to walk on eggshells, but they could live free to be kids. As time has gone on, I have slowly put these dreams aside. It is not that they have dissipated, but these dreams have taken a back seat. It started to become more painful to be honest. It felt so distant that it only made the longing hurt rather than bring excitement.

But recently these old dreams have been resurfacing. It could be because some of my good friends have just had babies. Or maybe I am thinking about it more because I am getting a bit older. I'm not sure what exactly is happening, but these dreams are coming up again. And it is crazy to think of being married and having babies. These desires of mine still feel just as far off, but they seem more possible somehow. It doesn't hurt anymore when I think about it. It feels foreign though. And I know the more people have babies around me, the more I will want my own. But I tell you all of this so that you do not let the seemingly impossible dream of having children and a family fade just because you are single now. Just because you are single does not mean you can't think of these things now. I may be very much a girl in these things, but I already have some baby names picked out, I dream about what my house will look like, I dream about how my husband will be as a father because if I don't, then I don't have vision for where I am headed and what God is trying to show me.

As women we long to be a wife and a mother, and there is nothing wrong with that. Sometimes I feel silly thinking of these things, but why should I? Just because I am single now doesn't mean I always will be. I have just as much of a right to dream of my future family as a woman who is married. And even if God never blesses us with biological children, there are plenty of children in the world who need mothers in their lives. Some children may even have a mother but be in need of a spiritual mother for a season. You never know how God will use the desire you have and how He will fulfill it. It is only a matter of time, and all we can do while we wait is to not lose hope. Hope will keep us afloat in this raging sea that life can be at times.

Take Advantage of This Season

With having dreams of marriage and family, we can often complain about not being there yet. But what we don't usually think about is how much work it is going to be. I don't know about you, but I love my time and space. I love having late mornings where I can wake up naturally, no alarm or human alarm to wake me up. I make my coffee, and I slowly ease into my day. I spend as much time as I want doing my devotions and praying. I can stay in my pajamas until the afternoon if I want. Obviously this does not happen as often as I would like it to, but it definitely happens more frequently than if I were to have a husband and kids.

I think when we are single, we don't think about how, if we were actually in a relationship and married, we have another person we have to plan around. We don't think about how someone else's schedule and feelings matter. To be honest, I am going to enjoy this time on my own. I love only having to plan around my schedule and what I want to do. I love doing what I want, when I want. We forget the luxury it is to be single. I see my married friends, and they don't have the freedom they once did or that I do. They now have to make someone else a priority other than just them self. I'm so happy I get this extended period of time. My singleness has been a lot longer than most of my friends, and I really believe that sometimes they envy the freedom I have. They would never say it out loud, well some would, and of course they are so happy to be with their men. But it is a whole different life than the one I have.

Right now, the whole world is open for me. I can go anywhere I want, when I want and not have to answer to anyone. This is a fun season to be in, and I think too often we wish we weren't in it when it truly is a gift. We have the rest of our lives to be married. I hated when people would say that to me when I was struggling so badly with being single. But it is true. Once we are married, it's done. That is it. No more being single, making decisions on your own, only thinking of yourself. You don't think you are selfish now, just wait until you are married and become *one*. Our flesh is going to be screaming and thinking of the days when it was just us. Ask anyone who is married, and they will tell you how true this really is.

Don't get me wrong; I can't wait to get married. But I am also pretty afraid because it will show me all my weaknesses and shortcomings when I need to constantly submit to someone else's needs above my own. That is what marriage is right? Putting someone above us. And when it is a healthy marriage, your husband will do the same with you. That is what makes a marriage balanced and whole. And when we have God in the middle of it, then it is possible. But for now, while you wait - be thankful for the time you have because pretty soon these years will be far behind you, and you will regret not taking advantage of this season you are living in.

26.

In the Wilderness

The last few years of my life, I have been in the wilderness. I am sure you have had one of those seasons as well or you may be in one right now. It is so challenging and difficult. My wilderness looked like a dry, barren wasteland filled with the unknown and a lot of quiet. I didn't think God was with me most of the time; He seemed so far away. And in the wilderness all I wanted was to not be alone. But there I was alone and sad. Every time I would have a little meltdown in my scarce season, the thing I wanted the most was a man. A man to hold me and tell me that everything would be okay. Little did I know, that is exactly what was happening except that the man I thought I wanted was not the one I got and not the one I really needed. I found God.

Now I knew God before this wilderness season, but I didn't know Him intimately. I saw Him as a far-off spirit who controlled my life and wasn't giving me what my heart desired. But in the wilderness I found love like I have never known before. I found love that brings me joy and fulfillment, peace and prosperity. I didn't know how much I was holding on with my own strength until I finally couldn't do it anymore, and I gave up. I let Him in, and it was the best thing that has ever happened to me. I finally saw Him there in the desert with me. He had been gently guiding me and showing me which way to go, so it could be just me and Him and no one else. He wanted me by myself so that He could whisper into my heart how much He loves me. He wanted to romance me and show me what a healthy, loving relationship is supposed to look like. So that when a man does come into my life, I will be ready for him.

I know now that God was waiting for me to give Him all of my heart before someone else could have any of it. It was frustrating most of the time because I didn't know how to give Him all of my heart. And I knew that was what was holding me back from my promise of a husband coming to pass. But the problem was that I was focusing too much on the promise itself and not the promise-giver. As soon as I shifted my focus and desires to Him, capital "H," and not him, I was able to find what I was looking for all along. I needed God's love to fully envelop my heart and take me on a journey of deeper intimacy with Him so that I could live in the fullness He had for me. I am still on the journey now, but I am much happier and am more in love with God than I ever have been.

Sometimes when I read His word, I begin to weep because of how much I love Him. I feel like I am walking around, looking at everything with rose-colored glasses, as if He created it just for me. This may sound conceited or like I am bragging, but I hope you hear this with the heart I am writing it in. Everyone can have a deep, loving relationship with God. Everyone can have a unique and special relationship with Him that is different from everyone else's. I myself did not understand that until recently. I found myself getting jealous of my friends who were having these amazing experiences with Jesus. The way they talked about Him made me more frustrated with my relationship with Him. I felt like a jealous girlfriend. Until one day, He broke me down and showed me that other people's experiences with Him do not take away from my relationship with Him.

I know a lot of the insecurity and jealousy with my relationship with God stemmed from my relationship with my earthly father. But I still could not shake it for so long, and it was a pattern in my life. But God is so gracious and loving that He wouldn't let me stay in that spot, but He slowly worked on my heart and challenged me to break free from that. I still want more of Him. I still want to know Him better. I want to spend more time with Him and have a closeness that I can't even explain in words. If you want this type of relationship with God, I encourage you to pray and ask Him for it. He will give it to you. It may take time and be painful along the way, but I promise you won't regret it.

I am Found

The more I get to know God, the more I am found. When I say I am found, I mean I am not lost. It is as simple as that. But the more I am found, the less I worry and stress about the unknowns of life. The more I am found, the more I love not only God, but the more I love people. The more I am found, the more free I am to do what I want because my desires are more in line with God's.

I think too often one of the reasons we so want to be in a relationship is because we are lost and just want something to focus on other than our worries and problems. At least that is how it used to be for me. But now that is not the case. A lot of it comes with time and maturing, but when God finds you, everything changes. He speaks to you about your purpose and what the point of life is. Some of the darkest times of my life are because I felt so lost. I tried to cling onto anything that would give me some sense of fulfillment. The more I find God and let Him find me, the more whole I become and the more I let go of the things that don't matter.

Being found means that you don't look to others for validation and assurance. This is very important before entering into a relationship because the more you know yourself and the more you are known by God, the less you look to a man to fulfill you and tell you who you are. It is a very dangerous place to be when you allow someone else to tell you who you are, especially if they are not a trustworthy, healthy person themselves. Many relationships fail because of how much pressure is put on someone when the other so needs their attention and reassurance. Of course in a healthy relationship there is still affirmation taking place, but your world won't come crashing down if that person does not give you the attention you are desperately seeking.

I truly believe that God sometimes does not give us our future husbands because He is waiting for us to get this. Over and over again people jump from relationship to relationship because they are seeking all the wrong things from all the wrong places. But I get it, our environments and culture will dictate what we want if we are not careful. We can only be found in a love that never leaves, or seeks to hurt, or rejects us. This love is unending, glorious, sweet, kind and gentle. Everything you have always dreamt of love being and more.

God Ordained

I think it is easy for us, especially in this area of waiting to meet our husband, to forget that God actually cares about who we marry, and He wants us to be married. At times it doesn't seem like it, since we know He could make it happen at any time if He really wanted. But hearing people's stories of how they met their loved one confirms to me that God is so in the midst of our love stories. He weaves together the stories of two people who are destined for one another. He creates these God-ordained moments without us even realizing it at the time. And that is the beauty of it, the mystery behind it all. We get frustrated with the unknown, but it's in the unknown that we are found and that our future husband is found as well.

It is in the dry, desert, wilderness seasons when things eventually come to life, and water springs forth from where there was none before. It is in this place where God changes us and brings us closer to Him. In the wilderness we feel lost and aimless, yet as we continue along this path through the seemingly endless wilderness, we eventually reach our destination only to realize we were there all along. When we are lost and alone, that is when God can come to our rescue and fill the places in our hearts that we long to be filled. He shows us how desired we are once we are alone with Him. Until He gets us alone, we are not able to find the intimacy we are so desperate for.

God knows exactly what He is doing. He knows your every second, every breath in this life, and He isn't going to lose you or abandon you. He has the perfect man for you. He won't be a perfect man, but he will be perfect for you. He is going to challenge you, frustrate you more often than not, and he will annoy you at times. But ultimately, you will love him like you have never loved anybody before. When God does make this God-ordained meeting take place, eventually everything will make sense. Why you had been single for so long, the why it didn't work out with that guy or that guy, the why you have been in this wilderness season as long as you have. The lonely nights and long days will all come crashing down and left with understanding and gratitude that everything does in fact happen for a reason.

God is mysterious and oh so wonderful, if we allow Him to be. He needs room to move and breathe in and through our lives. If we are constantly filling our lives jam-packed, when will He be able to show you what He actually has planned for us? His desire for us to be married is greater than our own. God loves giving us gifts, and if He could, He would pour all of them out onto us right this instant. But He knows the process we are in and what needs to take place before some things are handed over to us. And sometimes we need to realize we actually need to just reach out and grab it because He has already tried to give it to us. Allow the Holy Spirit to show you where you are at, in this and He will do the rest.

27.

Boys Are Confusing

How often have you heard from guys that girls are so confusing and that we don't know what we want? But I find that it is quite the opposite. I find that most girls do know what they want; they just can't seem to find it in the men they have encountered. Yet so often, especially in church, there are plenty of men who get so distracted by all the amazing women around them that they can't seem to choose. They flirt with any woman who will give them the attention they are so desperate to have. They will even go as far as seemingly pursuing a girl, when in fact they aren't at all.

For instance, recently there was a guy in my world who really had me confused. I didn't really know him, but a lot of my friends are friends with him. I quickly noticed him taking notice of me. He would tell me I looked beautiful when I would see him. He would rest his hand on my shoulder while standing behind me chatting with our friends. He would be extremely attentive to me: helping me up, making me coffee, giving me his jacket, etc. One time he even held my hand in both of his for a good few minutes while looking into my eyes and apologizing to me for making a silly mistake that really didn't bother me at all, but it was sweet that he cared. All of these little things kept adding up, and here I am thinking this guy is in love with me! I started to become interested which had me baffled, considering he is not really my type physically.

After a fun weekend as a group of friends, I figured he would definitely get my number. But no, he didn't. Then I hear from one of my girlfriends who is close to him that he has a few girls he is interested in and talking to. This had me in an uproar internally because I can't even count how many times this kind of situation has happened to me. You think a guy is into you, and the next thing you know, he was just interested in getting some attention and validation from a girl. Now I am not completely innocent myself when it comes to flirting with multiple guys, but it is never in a way that is crossing a line or even confusing to them (at least I hope not). But what makes it even worse is that these are the guys who complain how they want to be in a relationship and get married. Sometimes I just want to shake them and say *you do realize if you just chose a girl and pursued her and her only, that would happen!*

Now guys think we are the confusing ones. I am pretty sure if we are ready to be in a relationship, then if a guy pursued us the way we deserve and the way God intended, we would be "theirs." Of course other things need to align as well such as morals and values, and there needs to be some attraction and chemistry. To me it is not that complicated. But Christians have made it so complicated. We have even become technical and critical when it comes to our calling compared to theirs. Back in the day, I don't think they even thought much about that, and God made it happen anyway. I think our generation needs to know everything we possibly can before taking a risk. But that diminishes it as a risk altogether. Love and relationships always involve a risk and a decision to be made. I'm not sure where things changed and why, but until people understand that love is a decision, healthy relationships cannot flourish. You see someone you like, you get to know him or her, and you pursue a relationship. Obviously easier said than done, but I truly believe it does not have to be so complicated and confusing.

When men are confusing and I think they like me, it is easy for me to get carried away in my head and heart. But I am still learning to remind myself that if a guy is worth it, he will pursue me. He has to make the first move, not even just the first but also the first few. Until it is very apparent that he wants to be in a relationship, then there is no point in even entertaining the idea. And the most obvious way for a guy to make it known that he is interested and pursuing with purpose is by simply telling you. If a guy can't tell you straight up that he likes you and wants to pursue a relationship with you, then move on until he does something about it. And if he never does anything about it, then he isn't right for you.

28.

Social Pressures

If being married were not the ideal in life, I would not mind being single as much. If it was more of the norm to be single, especially in the Christian world in your later twenties and up, I would not think as often about one day when I'm married. Honestly I see my friends married and in relationships, and it is sweet and looks fun, but I have realized how much I have loved being single. I love having me time. And additionally, if it weren't increasingly difficult to get pregnant once you hit thirty, I would be in no rush at all.

Even so I don't feel too rushed at this stage of my life. Yes, I really want it to happen, but part of me gets so nervous thinking about it. I mean, my life will have to change so much. I will have to be in constant communication with someone. Right now I sometimes don't answer my phone when my friends are calling me, and

I can leave a text till the next day. But once I am in a relationship, I won't be able to do that. The thought of it makes me cringe a little.

But then I think of all the things I do that will be so much more fun with someone I love. Like road trips for instance. Right now I am sitting at my friend's place up in northern California in their cute home in the woods where there is peace and quiet. I drove up here on my own, and it was fun, but it also would have been more memorable with my future man. Still if it was not viewed as the better of the two, I probably would not even think about it. I would do my thing, happy and content, not knowing what I am missing out on. I still don't even know what I a missing out on considering I have never gotten past the awkward dating stage where you don't know where it is headed, until it just dies, and you move on. It isn't that I haven't liked any of the guys I have dated, a few of them I have liked a lot. But that doesn't mean they were right for me. I know I scared a few of them away whether it was out of intimidation or I was too much for them to handle. But either way, they weren't it and I praise God for that.

Too often people are getting into relationships with the wrong person. I think when we feel pressure, it is easy for us to settle or choose poorly based on someone's looks or income. People's perceptions of us tend to hold too much regard in our lives. People want us to conform to what is comfortable for them because if you don't, it makes them take a good hard look into their own lives. When you try to go outside the box of the culture you live in, people question you and judge your point of view.

God did not call us to fit the 'norm.' He has called us to go against the grain and carve nuances into the world and to break barriers. Many people aren't happy being single and weren't happy until they met their spouse, so they project that onto their single friends thinking they aren't actually happy on their own. So they take matters into their own hands and decide to play cupid. Sometimes it does work out, and they genuinely do want you to be happy especially if they have seen you struggle in your singleness before. But if you are content where you are at, let them know and set boundaries. You may need to tell some friends and family to back off and not to worry because you aren't worried yourself.

It does get hard when you feel the pressure to meet someone, and many times the pressure can come from yourself. I know I have put plenty of pressure on myself especially as I get older and quickly approach the dreaded thirty. I say dreaded because in today's society thirty and single is just not something you want to be, not in church standards. In the world there is a little more time because it is expected that you sleep around while you wait for Mr. Right because somehow that makes it easy (hint of sarcasm). But sex, not with the right person and within the bounds marriage, can be heartbreak hell.

Comparison

It has almost been a whole two months since a new year has started. I don't feel my life is where I want it to be, but when do I ever? I have a problem comparing myself to others. It is a disease that infects the most willing hearts. Honestly, I rarely feel like my life is good enough, and somehow I think that if I were married at least I would have that to feel some sense of security and assurance in life. But how sad is that. I know that it isn't true. I know that being married will only highlight all my flaws all the more. We all face this in some form or another. It is human nature and our fleshy ways that scream at us about being better than someone else. We crave it whether we admit it or not.

Ever since I can remember, I have silently, subconsciously compared myself, and my life, to everyone around me. I usually never let it seep out into my friendships and relationships. But it is there, and it makes me so unhappy with where my life is. Because when I see everyone around me has lives looking way "cooler" or better than mine, I think my life sucks. What is even sadder is that people probably look at my life and think the same thing. It is this vicious cycle that allows for no one to be truly happy. And I am sure some of you reading truly are happy about where you are in life, but I am also sure that there is something trying to grab your attention about something you don't have yet, such as a man or a marriage, a baby or a job.

I start believing that I am not good enough or worthy enough to have the life I so desperately want. And even once I get it, will I appreciate it? I know I will be tempted to compare it to the built-up idea, fantasy, dream that I thought it was going to be. My idealism can have a way of holding me back from accepting reality for what it is or rather what I think it should be. But how unfair to do to myself or anyone else. How will I ever get married when I am waiting around for this "perfect" man to appear and sweep me off of my feet? But for some reason I can't let "him" go. Now logically I know he isn't going to be perfect. I know he will have many flaws as I do. But is it so wrong to believe there is someone out there who is "perfect" for me?

I am such a dreamer to the point that I feel none of my dreams will ever come true because I am already thinking up my next dream before the first has come to pass. Yet here I am just sitting and not doing anything with my dreams. But then when I really think about it, I have accomplished a lot of dreams of mine. I moved to another country, and I am in the process of writing this book. Two dreams down and another thousand to go! My biggest dream has been to write and publish books in hopes that they will help someone. Reading has been my saving grace throughout my life because it has taught me so much. You may be thinking, "Why am I reading this girl's thoughts on being single when she is still single? She obviously doesn't know what she is talking about." Ok maybe you hadn't thought that until I just said it. But what better person to write about being single than someone who is single themselves? And not only am I single now, I have been single my whole life. I mean that is pretty impressive and basically makes me an expert at this point. You may think that is pathetic, and honestly I think it is too sometimes. But I want to help people, especially women, in this area. I don't want others struggling in their single-ness the way I have. I don't want us to compare ourselves to everyone else and think we are less than because we are single.

It sucks that our society dictates these beliefs and thoughts on social norms, but let's make a new norm where single is not looked at as a sad way to live, but it is looked at as fulfilled and happy. The desire to be in a relationship may never fully leave, but don't let it. It is there for a reason, and in the right season it will happen. Your happily ever after will happen, probably not how you pictured it happening, but it will happen all the more. But until then, let's start living out some of our dreams and don't let comparison slip into our heads and hearts. We are created for more than to live unhappily with where we are in life. We have our best days ahead of us.

Take the Help

I remember I used to have such a hard time with letting people help me. It was definitely an issue of mine due to many different reasons. But as I grew and changed, I slowly let people help me. What was the hardest was letting men help me, especially single ones because I felt like I owed them something since they weren't my boyfriend and didn't have to help me. I wanted to be viewed as independent and not needing anyone. But eventually I learned that me allowing others to help me, especially men, only helps my future relationship as well. Relationships and marriage are a partnership. You help each other and carry the weight of life or more literally the groceries (unless he can carry them all).

But even in my life right now, I am still single as you know, recently moved back to California from living in Australia for two years, and I have definitely needed some help. I have been staying with some of my married friends because they have the room and wanted to help me out. They aren't charging me because they want me to get back on my feet. I know what some of you may be thinking, it sounds pathetic. I would have thought that too in the past. But now I look at it as a blessing and opportunity. I am not only living in a beautiful home for free, but I also get to be around married couples and see how they do life together. I am learning, and it is only preparing me for what is ahead. I never thought I would be in this position, and if you had told me 10 years ago that this is what my life would look like, I probably would have been mortified. But God has taken my pride and transformed me into someone who looks at life so differently and especially looks at being single with different eyes.

The last two years is where I really learned to take help from men and not feel like I owe them anything. The Bible College I attended is where I really learned this lesson. There is a weekly women's event called *Sisterhood* where women are empowered to live up to their potential and live out the calling on their life. At these weekly events the men would serve the ladies: greet them at the door, make coffee, help set up everything including doing all the heavy lifting, open doors, and chivalry is definitely not dead there. These acts didn't just stay at the women's weekly event, but the men of the college would continue doing such kind, gentlemanly acts throughout the week at college. At first it made me uncomfortable to be honest, only because I had never experienced anything quite like it. But God used these men to slowly chip away at my slightly-hardened-towards-men heart.

I now gladly take the help of men and have continued to be treated with respect and dignity. Some of the men in my life have really changed my outlook and perspective on men in general. It is so beautiful when you let people help you. It not only blesses you, but it blesses them too. It causes you to help others more, and it is a full circle of blessings for many.

29.

Awareness

Self-awareness brings freedom. I think oftentimes people are so terrified to see their own faults and think that if they do, it will bring the opposite of freedom. But like the Bible says *the truth will set you free.* When you know the things that are holding you back or keeping you from living life to the fullest, that is when you can break free from them. Only once you are aware of something, can it change. If you struggle to see who you really are or even if you are afraid to see your strengths and weaknesses, pray that the Holy Spirit would show you. He will never condemn you or make you feel bad about these things, but He will show you where He can help you transform more into the person He has created you to be.

Once you start on your awareness journey, it will help you choose the right person for you. Knowing yourself better only allows you to see more clearly if someone is right or wrong for you. You will no longer settle for mediocre, but you will be more sure of what you want and will not waver in that. Be sure to choose someone who is also self-aware, otherwise it will create conflict down the road. That is not to say that you won't ever have conflict with someone who is aware, but it will be easier to navigate and work through conflict with someone who is in touch with their own thoughts and feelings.

Walls Up

Past experiences of heartbreak can teach us how to build walls around our heart. Not physical walls, but metaphorically speaking - walls that keep people out and keep our emotions in. Some walls can be built up so high and so thick that it would take a wrecking ball to make even a dent. So often these walls of protection only keep us away from potential love and goodness. There are different levels and extremes with how self-protected a person can be. I think the worst yet best part of having these walls up is that the right people can see through them. I used to have so many walls up, and honestly I probably still have some up even now. They have changed a bit though. They used to not let anyone in. I didn't want anyone, especially men, to see who I was. Now I have some independent walls up, just so men and everyone knows that I am good on my own, and I don't need anybody.

I have some friends with walls up too. We are all still single. And many people think that if we just didn't have our walls up, then we could meet someone. See, walls scare guys. Walls can easily bring out their own insecurities, and many guys are not ready for that. I say guys because men are not afraid of walls. I have a friend; we will call her Sarah, who recently was asked out on a date multiple times by the same guy. He sees her walls and has called her out on it in a loving way. He sees her self-protection and independence, but it makes him more interested in her and willing to take a chance. That is a man!

Now on the other hand, Sarah has another guy in her life that she has been interested in. But he has been extremely confusing to her, flirting one-minute, and then the next he is ignoring her or avoiding her. He too is aware of her walls, but instead of talking to her about it, has said something to Sarah's brother-in-law. He continues to play games because he is interested, yet so afraid of the walls she may have because he doesn't know if he has it in him to push through them. Now of course I am just speculating. Who is to say if I am completely right in this situation? But honestly I have seen it before in my own life. The worst part about it is that the second guy who plays games is the one it could actually work out with if he would just get it together! I speak from experience in my own life. I told Sarah she needs to call this guy out or he will continue to play games with her. This will reveal if he is ready to be a man or not.

A man will not shy away from a challenge. Walls can definitely be challenging, and I truly believe that even if you do have walls up, a man will fight for you regardless. He isn't going to care that you have been heartbroken and now are afraid to love again. He will understand where you are at and be patient with you. The right man will think you are worth the wait. He will choose you, not because of what you can give him, but what he can give you. So if you have some walls up and are frustrated that you can't seem to break them down, I wouldn't worry about it too much if I were you. You want to be with someone who is going to do whatever he can to be with you. And if a guy hasn't come along and done so thus far, then he wasn't right for you. And if you are still single, then it must not be the right time, and maybe your walls need to be broken down a bit before someone else comes and finishes them off. God is the ultimate wall-wrecker. One touch of Holy Spirit can wreck you for the better and change your life forever.

If you are currently dating a guy with some walls up and you truly believe he is the one for you, keep praying for him and for both of you, that God would protect your hearts and guide you. Not everyone's story is the same, and sometimes guys are the ones who have heartbreak that needs to be mended. You may need to let him go before it can work out. But time will tell whether he is in fact the right person for you. Trust God, keep fighting for your dream man, and don't give up.

Guard Your Heart

Guard your heart; we have heard it time and time again. We know the verse, Proverbs 4:23 NLT, "Guard your heart above all else, for it determines the course of your life." But how do we guard our hearts without putting up walls that keep us from falling in love? How do we let ourselves be interested and guard our hearts at the same time? I think it is a lot easier to do than we think.

To guard your heart does not mean you cannot have feelings for someone. It does not mean that you cannot share your heart with someone you are interested in. But what it does mean is that you open up to someone without letting them fully in. Deep intimacy is for a husband and a wife, the type of intimacy where you know someone inside and out. Guarding your heart looks like you protecting yourself and not getting your security from another person or relationship. Rather than putting your heart into the hands of someone else, you put your heart into the hands of God who will keep it from harm and who can restore any brokenness that might seep in.

There is a huge difference between being guarded and guarding. Guarded is when you will not let anyone in whatsoever because you are letting fear dictate your life. I have been very guarded in the past. If anyone showed any interest in me, even if I was interested in them, I would push them away. I did not believe that they actually cared for me, and I thought they just wanted to use me for what they wanted and move on when they were done. Experience and observation showed me this to be true. But it wasn't the truth; I made it my truth. Because that is what I believed, I only went for the ones who didn't truly care for me, so I could prove my truth was right. But it was a lie. There are men out there who will truly care. They won't just want you because you are pretty or because you have a nice body. But they will want you for your heart, for who you are and not what you can do for them.

True love is sacrificial. True love is when you think more about what the other person wants and needs more than your own. And when both parties in a relationship have that belief and outlook, then true love can prevail and all is right in the world. Unfortunately more often than not, this is not the case in many relationships. People let their selfishness get the best of them, and they start thinking about what they are getting out of it. This is when relationships take a turn for the worst, and people do not last with their previous commitment. This is why it is so important to guard your heart above all else.

When you put too much pressure on a relationship and onto your partner, it puts strain on them, and problems arise. When you are able to guard your heart by giving yourself and relationship to God, then that pressure is not on your partner any longer. The pressure is given to Jesus, and He is the only one who can handle that. He has done it before on the cross. He has proven himself able, so we can go to him with anything and everything. Humans were not created to be able to handle or carry that kind of weight on their own. That is why we need to be in relationship with Him in order for our other relationships to be at ease.

What happens when we do not guard our heart is that our lives go off course and become a mess. When our hearts are not guarded and then become hurt and jaded, we start making decisions based on the wrong lens. Our lens becomes clouded with bitterness, anger, and resentment. We start to look at everyone through this lens without realizing we are even doing it. We don't see the smudge marks that need to be cleaned from the lens, so we can see more clearly and accurately. No, we just start to squint through the filth and take a guess at what we are looking at rather than knowing exactly what it is we are seeing. Jesus can become our lens when we admit that we have been hurt and that we didn't guard our hearts properly. Jesus can only protect us when we let him, which is through obedience. When we are not obeying him, we take away his right to protect and guard our hearts that leaves us vulnerable to getting hurt. And I am speaking from experience from times when I was not obedient.

The good news is that even if you have been disobedient and you see that now, Jesus will forgive you and guard and protect your heart once again. And this time, He will teach you how to do it. He will not leave you hanging. And then when you look back, though you were hurt before, you can now see that Jesus was really there protecting you all along from your life totally going off track. He lets you make your own decisions and mistakes, but He won't let you go too far without helping you get back to where you need to be. Thank God!

30.

Date with Intent to Marry

I believe dating should be with the intention to marry. I know many people just date to have fun, and there is nothing wrong with that other than someone's feelings will eventually get hurt. Not only will someone get hurt, but also it can cause much confusion between both parties. Especially as a Christian, I believe dating should be very intentional. I am not sure where you stand on sex before marriage, but I am "old school" in my beliefs, and I believe we should wait until we are married. Have I stuck to that in my past? No, so no judgment here if that is not your belief or your journey. But either way, this belief alone changes what dating looks like. Obviously waiting to have sex can be very challenging. This does not mean we should rush into marriage because we can't control ourselves. I think the longer we wait in our singleness, the quicker the process can be when dating, being engaged and getting married. The longer you have to wait, the longer you have to learn about who you are and what you like. The older you are, the more transparent and direct you will be when dating. I know for me I am much more bold in the way I handle situations with guys than when I was in my early twenties. Everyone's story is different, and there is nothing wrong with waiting years in a relationship before getting married or only knowing one another a few months before the big day.

Being intentional though is key to a relationship working out. This goes for both you and the man. It is hard to know from a first date if you are going to marry someone or not. Some people do know right away while others it may take a lot more time. But having the intention that you are looking for a life partner and not just your next fling will help save you time and emotions. Being clear from the get-go is key to making that happen. Obviously you don't want to freak a guy out by being overly enthusiastic about getting married. But you can explain to them that you are looking for something more serious and a relationship that will lead to marriage. And if they get scared and run off, then you know they weren't for you anyway. If a man gets scared of commitment like that, then they aren't ready to commit. You can save time by laying it all out there, and if he runs, he isn't the man for you.

Men may think they want to get married, but when it comes down to it, they aren't actually ready. And that is okay. There are men out there who are ready, and they will prove themselves true of that as time goes on when they are still there by your side. Now he may be scared to commit, and your potential relationship may be much slower and more confusing than you hoped for. But if he is still sticking around and wanting to get to know you, then maybe give him some more time. Ultimately you need to trust your heart on when to move on and when to stay, and the Holy Spirit will guide you in that. But you want to both want the same things in life or it really has no room to go anywhere.

Online Dating and Dating Apps

Online dating has quickly taken a rise from being just a second chance at love for widowers and divorcees to now being the new norm for all ages. Not only are there countless dating websites, there are now multiple dating apps that are easy access on your phone. Swipe left or right, and you are that much closer to finding a connection. But what happened to chivalry? Is it really dead after all?

It is now so easy and convenient that a guy can ask a girl out through a quick direct message. Not only that, there are even some dating apps where the girl is to contact the guy (Bumble), mostly to avoid inappropriate messages from guys they don't want to be talking to anyway. But the whole idea of it has me wondering where is the romance in it all? What about the beautiful love stories that start out with a timely first meeting where fate and destiny brought them together? Call me cheesy, idealistic, and a starry-eyed dreamer, but these types of meetings do take place between a man and a woman or we would never have movies about it. Yes, obviously movies are dramatized and definitely unrealistic most of the time, but some of their ideas must have originated from true stories. Besides movies, I am sure you have heard some pretty great love stories from friends or if no one your age, maybe grandparents because back in the day they knew how to woo a girl.

Call me old-fashioned, but I still think we can have those kinds of romances. It won't be perfect all the time, and it will probably be frustrating in the beginning stages, but that is all part of the writing on a good story. I think it is great that there is not such a negative view or stigma on online dating at this point. And I am not saying it is wrong if you do it. I myself am on a dating app when I never thought I would actually try it. I have found for me that it helps pass the time and teaches me what I want and what I don't want in a man. It has helped me be more open minded, but it has also taught me to stick to my standards and not compromise.

Are you trying to make this happen in your own strength? Are you actively seeking it and trying to make it happen because you are too impatient to wait for God to bring him into your life? What if your man was right around the corner, and you are just wasting your time and efforts with someone who isn't even for you? I don't think we need to actively seek dating someone to find the right one. I believe that if you just live your life to the full - whatever that may look like for you - and enjoy yourself, at the perfect time the right guy will appear in your life whether it is at a coffee shop while you get your morning coffee, at church on a Sunday, or on a dating app. It may be more random than that, and we won't know until it happens, but I truly believe God has it covered for each and every one of us.

I think if anything, it can be a great experience in practicing dating, getting to know someone and learning about yourself in the process. At first I was so against dating apps, but I decided I should try them for myself since I have been some what passing judgment on something I really knew nothing about. My experience with it has not produced anything lasting as of yet. It definitely is not my ideal, and my old soul cringes, but this is the way things are going in this day and age.

In saying all that, I do believe He can use online dating to bring you your husband if that is what is best for you. I can't tell you what is right or wrong in this area. But these are just some of my thoughts on it. For example, since I was young, I have always desired to meet my husband in an unexpected way without me seeking it. I have always desired that he would pursue me like I have never been pursued before in a way that only God could orchestrate. For me, I am not ready, and I don't think I will ever be to let go of those dreams because I believe God put them there, and He will fulfill it in due time. I have to be patient and trust and live my life not consumed with the unending question of "when, God, when?"

Online dating does work for some, I have known couples to meet through the different dating apps and websites, and they really do suit each other and love one another. I have seen great things come from it. I think that if you do decide to move forward with it that the best way to do online dating is to know where you stand on your boundaries, beliefs and morals. Don't make any shift in them to fit someone else's standards because if you do, it probably won't work out and you won't be happy. Your standards and beliefs are who you are. And don't waste your time or someone else's. But this goes for any dating, whether you met online or not.

Texting

I prefer texting over talking on the phone…most of the time. Does anyone else hate the beginnings of a potential relationship when texting can be so nerve-racking? Do I text him? Do I wait for him to text me? Should I say that…no, that's too forward. Ugh I hate the over analyzing that tends to happen when I have a crush on someone. You ask your girlfriends what they think before you send it, and they make you feel like an idiot because of what you were going to say. Or you aren't coming across that you are interested enough. Texting can be so misread too. Just the thought of it is stressing me out.

But honestly at this stage in my journey, I don't find it so daunting. Maybe it is because I am so sick and tired of caring so much and over-thinking things. I now have this mentality that if he doesn't like what I am saying, then he isn't right for me. There are plenty of guys out there believe it or not. I know it does not always seem like it, and the ones actually worth paying attention to are few and far between. But they are out there, and we don't need to hold so tightly to one thinking he is the only one there will ever be.

I get it though, as humans we want to make a good impression. We don't want to be misunderstood. That is why sometimes I think a phone call is much better than a text. And God bless the men who will call you rather than just text you all the time. I do have to admit though when you are interested in someone, and they text you morning till night, it is nice. It is nice to know they are thinking about you, and they want to be talking to you even if it can't be in person. But then there are those "serial texters" who only just text you but never actually want to hang out. I had a few of those in the past. I never understood that. But I think some people just like any kind of attention they can get, and it somehow makes them feel better.

Just a tip though, be careful with texting too much in the beginning. Save some conversation for face-to-face interaction. You will have more to talk about and will get to know someone on a much deeper level. I know this is the day and age we are living in, but I think the more you can keep texts short and sweet, keeps the mystery alive and keeps them wanting more. They will eventually get it that you aren't much of a "texter" and they will want to get you in person. But if they don't, then you may have to move on.

31.

It's a Mystery

Today I went on a walk by the beach on one of my favorite beach trails. It's 2.3 miles of ocean-lined trail in south Orange County, San Clemente - to be exact. It was a beautiful day as I drove down to the beach, but as I got closer I saw some fog rolling in. I decided it would still be beautiful and went on my way. As I looked out across the ocean and fog, there was an eerie feeling with the mist almost hiding the surfers that were trying to catch a wave. Further out into the distance were some rocks poking out of the water. It didn't look like sunny California, but more like the east coast or Oregon coast with its little bit of chill.

This beautiful, rare scene had me thinking about mystery. Looking out into the grey abyss and stretching my eyes as far as I could see, had me daydreaming about what is out there. I imagined pirate ships far out at sea, filled with treasure and wonder. It also made me think about my future husband. Why you might ask? I really have no idea. Maybe he will look like a pirate? I doubt it, but it made me think about the mystery and excitement that it is, waiting for him to appear. As if he was hidden behind that grey fog just waiting to be found or more so he is waiting to find me, the coastline…the land…his treasure. It is like I am here stranded on land, and he is out there stranded at sea. We both are stretching to see where the other might be. I know this is kind of cheesy and a romantic thought, but those thoughts can be very comforting at times.

I mean here I am, back in America from living in Sydney, just a few miles from where I grew up and lived most of my life, and not much about that sounds very romantic to me. I had dreamt of meeting someone while in Sydney. Yesterday, I went to an interview for a possible dream job and found myself sitting with girls who are a bit younger than me. And when I say younger, they just graduated college. When I told them I just moved back from Sydney, they looked at me wide-eyed with excitement. And of course one of the first questions about my experience there was if I met an Australian love while I was there. I had to burst their bubble and tell them no with a disappointing tone.

But today when I went on my beach walk, I let myself be wide-eyed once more. Though it is hard to imagine how or when it will happen, looking at my circumstances. I still dare to believe that he is out there, maybe lost at sea, figuratively speaking of course. He is searching through the haze surrounding him, straining his eyes to find me, his long lost treasure. And I believe the same is for you. Your "pirate" is using his compass and map, changing the direction of his sails while the wind pushes him forward towards his dream come true that is found in the woman that you are. So let it be a mystery for now and dare to dream in the vastness that is the sea. He will come, just as you can't look any longer, while the sun begins to burn off the density that once made it impossible to see what was ahead.

Let Him Find You

The other weekend I went to my friend's church that was recently planted in Los Angeles. It was incredible and reminded me of "home." It was Valentine's Day, and I went with my best guy friend. I know what you're thinking, he is one of your best friends and he is a guy...isn't the point to marry your best friend?! Normally I would say yes, but you know when you are actually just best friends and you cannot imagine being in a romantic relationship? That is us, strictly friends. Anyway, that was just a side note. The pastors, husband and wife, spoke on one of the points together in the message. His wife highlighted Proverbs 31:10 NLT:

> "Who can find a virtuous and capable wife?
> She is more precious than rubies."

I love this because when she spoke on this verse, she emphasized that it says "WHO can find her?" meaning that we are not to go looking, but he (our future husbands) will find us. All we need to do is become the virtuous and capable woman we were created to be. But it is hard for women, because of our need and want to control things, to sit back and not go chasing after what we want. Oftentimes we want to plot and ploy about how to make things happen and because we are efficient, we want to do it quicker than most men can. Because obviously there isn't much sense of urgency in many men these days to go out and find a Proverbs 31 type of woman who is more precious than rubies. I mean, we are still single, aren't we?

Seriously though, when I heard her speak and tell about how their story unfolded, it was confirmation to me not that I don't need to go out and look for it; waiting will pay off in the right time. If you are feeling discouraged in your waiting right now, be encouraged that it is not for nothing, you will meet the right guy for you, and it will pay off in the end. For whatever reason, you are still waiting, but God has the perfect timing and person for you. It will be beautiful, exciting, and a happy time. It will also be challenging and life-changing in the best possible way. Pray for patience and fulfillment during your wait and watch God's faithfulness revealed in due time.

32.

It Happens out of Nowhere

We have all heard it before, and I've talked about it in earlier chapters, it will happen when you least expect it. But even more than that, it happens out of nowhere. It is as if this "Mr. Right" appears out of thin air! I have not experienced it yet, but I have seen it for my friends and have heard beautiful stories of how people meet. Now we still are called to do our part, by being open and available and growing while we wait, but when God sees that it is the right time for you and him, then it can happen suddenly. God loves to move and work in the "suddenlys" in life not just in love, but also in opportunities, blessings and miracles, and this is no different.

God works in mysterious ways. But really it only looks mysterious to those who do not know Him. When it is right, He makes it pretty clear that it is. He may make it happen very fast, but really to the person it is happening to, it doesn't seem fast at all because of all the years, moments and tears that led them there to that *suddenly* moment. God is not some puzzle to solve or code to crack, He will make it clear when the time is right and when things align if we let go and let Him do His thing.

I have always believed in this kind of story of how I meet the man of my dreams. And for many others in the same way, where God drops him into your life at the perfect time. Maybe not as fast or in the way you thought He would. But in the out-of-nowhere kind of way, where there are too many random things in common or similar desires of the heart. That is if you let it. What I mean is, I think many people sometimes grow impatient in waiting; they let frustration and loneliness take over which causes them to settle for something less than what they were meant to have. I have been guilty of this or at least guilty of trying to settle, but thank God He never let me. This can be in all areas of life, not just in the relationship department. Some people do not even realize they are settling. You know if you are settling or not by discerning if you have peace about a person or situation. In order to not settle, you must be aware of your lack of peace and not ignore it and let it reside in you to where it has become a part of you. You settle when you let big standards or dreams go for someone. If it is the right person, you will not have to let go of standards and certain dreams because he will meet those expectations. For example if you are expecting him to look identical to Ryan Gosling, chances are that is not going to happen. But you will be even more attracted to him because of who he is to you. That is the beauty of love and relationships centered on God. If you can keep God at the heart of things, you will continue to grow in your attraction and love for that person no matter how they look in comparison to others. And it won't matter to you because you both are meant to be together.

So wait for your "suddenly" moment that will be almost too good to believe because it is that good. Don't settle for second best because it isn't what God has for you anyway. He has the best guy specifically for you, and if you hold out for him, it will be well worth it.

Helpful Tips to Know If He is Right For You

We have talked about many topics so far. The frustrations, knowing if you are ready, what to do while you wait, but we haven't talked about what we should look for when we do meet a potential love? We have talked about some already like, "You'll know when you know." But to be more specific, something helpful is praying that when you see him you will know. We have heard it before, love at first sight. Or "he knew when he saw her, he wanted to marry her." Sometimes it could be plain old physical attraction that makes someone utter those words. But I also believe God can cause someone to declare something like that. For example, I have always prayed that my future husband would know when he saw me that I was the one for him. It happened to my Dad when he first saw my mom. I want him to know before I do so that he will pursue me right away, rather than me having to be confused and frustrated for months before anything happens. It may sound crazy, but I know this has happened for people. When we are specific in our prayers about our future husband, it helps us figure out if someone is for us or know much quicker. It may not look like how we imagined it to, but we will get confirmation and peace if they are the right person for us.

Another helpful tip for deciding if someone is a good match for you is if they make you a better person. Do you feel like yourself around them? Do you feel confident and like you can share your thoughts and feelings with that person? If you do not have that experience with the person, then they probably aren't right for you. Now this doesn't mean you won't have any nerves or butterflies in your stomach; it is normal to feel a little excited or nervous around the man of your dreams. I mean, you have been waiting a long time for him to arrive, so when he finally does, it is just a little overwhelming in the best way. But whether you lack peace when being with him is the key indicator. Does he build you up and encourage you? If he doesn't, then I suggest moving on.

Another way to know if he is right for you is by asking if your friends and family like him. I know sometimes friends and family can be the opposite of helpful in some life-changing things. But if the majority of your friends and family don't like him, then that really tells you there is something not right. If he does not get along with your people, then it is not going to make for a healthy, long-lasting relationship.

Does he put you first before others and other things? If he is not putting you as one of his top priorities, especially over his "boy's nights," then what makes you think that is going to change once you are married? If it isn't boy's nights that will keep him away, it will be work or a hobby or whatever else that could put a strain on your relationship. It is good for a potential husband to have friends and a hobby, for sure, but you want to make certain it doesn't take up the majority of his free time. If he doesn't want to make time for you and spend time with you, then that is a huge indicator something is not right.

Some of these things will not be very easy to see at first. And hopefully it won't take too much time to see it because you don't want to waste time or energy. But if you are being true to yourself and firm in your standards and convictions, you shouldn't have trouble seeing if someone is right for you or not. It will be hard at times because your desire for it to work out may color your perspective that is why it is important to be honest with yourself as much as possible. And don't allow him too many chances. I have made that mistake before, but the right guy won't make you have to. He is going to do what he says he will do, no excuses. And obviously sometimes things come up, but if those things are coming up more often than not it is time to move on.

Sometimes we confuse attraction and chemistry as the right thing. And unfortunately, those things are hard to come by, so when we do, we want it to work so badly. But I have found that it is definitely not everything. I think we need those things initially, but ultimately what is their character like? Do their actions back up their words? This is huge and so rare to find. We want the total package, and we will get it if we wait. The right guy for you is going to look so different than any other guy you have ever been involved with. Not physically different, though that may be the case too, but he will treat you differently than you have ever been treated. But don't stop there because you need to make sure he has the other things as well. Does he check all the "boxes" and more? Not literal boxes, but there are things God has planted in your heart for a reason to help you navigate whether someone is right for you or not. Listen to those things when you meet someone, and do not stop looking for them. If you aren't finding them, then move on. I know we want to linger with that person and hope they eventually meet our expectations, but the reality is that they probably won't. The right person and the right timing will be so apparent and clear, so if you are not having that experience, then let it go and keep seeking God.

We Need Validation

As women we need validation. It is the way we are wired. When we get validation from a man, we are unstoppable. I think men need just as much validation, but in a different way than women. What I struggle with is that when a man seems to be a possible fit for me, they need more validation from me than I'm receiving from them. It is a two-way street here, and I feel like we are only going one way. This has to do with my personality too though. I tend to validate people to the expense of my own needs until I run pretty dry and need major pouring into. This is not a good way to live, and it isn't healthy. But I am working on it!

The right guy will be a man who validates you, and you won't need to ask for it. He will validate you without you saying anything. You won't question where you both are at because he will bring it up. He will tell you he likes you before you tell him. He will say I love you first. He won't have you spinning out of control with questions and uncertainties; you will know where he stands. This is what a man does, one who is confident and secure in whom he is. They are definitely hard to come by, but he will be worth the wait. There are many great men out there, but are you willing to wait for the right one?

When you do find this type of man, make sure to validate him as well. He may be secure and all of that, but he will still need and want to hear how great he really is. Maybe words of affirmation isn't his love language, maybe it is touch or acts of service. Whatever it is (you can take a free quiz online, and I highly recommend the book, *The Five Love Languages* by Gary Chapman), validate him through his love language, not yours. And he will need to do the same with you. Everyone feels love differently, and it is so helpful when you can know and understand how your significant other accepts and gives love. Most marriages today end in divorce because neither one of them is giving the other love the way they desire it.

Validating and loving someone takes hard work and persistence. At first it may seem fairly easy being in the "honeymoon" phase of a relationship. Not to compare a relationship to a job, but it is similar in the way when you get a new job. At first you absolutely love it, and a few months down the line, the magic has slowly dissipated, and you are left with just a means to make money unless you work at loving your job again. A relationship takes effort. When things start to get boring or mundane with a person, you have to create ways to bring it to life again like going on an adventure or going to a new restaurant you both have wanted to try. And when you are married, it is the same thing. You will need to spice up the relationship by making an effort or else you will dig yourself into a hole that will be much harder to get out of, the deeper in it you go.

Follow the Leader

In today's society, most women consider themselves feminists. Back in the day, women did not lead or even speak in churches. Women could not be the CEO of a major company. Women were put in a box of housekeepers and cooks. But nowadays, we can pretty much do whatever we want. I think this is incredible! Women are amazing, strong, and powerful, and I am all for us being a *Wonder Woman*. But with saying that, I think it is so important to not only lead, but to also follow.

Because women are now able to be leaders, I think it has given many men permission to sit back and become more passive, obviously this is not all men. But I do see it in some relationships, and we have all heard someone say, "Well she wears the pants in that relationship." I don't know about you, but I never want someone to say that about my future relationship. The man should lead in a relationship. It is Biblical. But it is also dangerous when you are with the wrong man. If you are with a man who does not have a strong relationship with God, then he is going to have a hard time not taking advantage of his leadership role or he will have a hard time taking the leadership role within the relationship. If a man does not have a relationship with God and is not relying on Him for help, he will feel way too much pressure in leading.

Now obviously I have seen great, healthy leadership in men who are not in a relationship with God. I personally do not know how they do it because for me I tried living and doing things without following God, and it never went well for me. But I do know nonbelievers who are able to take the lead in their relationships, but I also see how it could be even better for them if they relied on God.

Men were created to take the lead in our relationships, and when you give them that role and respect, watch how they grow in confidence in that. If you are at the beginning stages of dating someone who is not taking the lead after giving them multiple opportunities to, consider moving on. It isn't that they will never get there, but you don't have time to waste. And if you are truly meant to be with them, God will make it happen and whip them into shape. But you do not have to sacrifice your time and energy trying to help them along because you will then be doing that for the rest of your relationship. You have not waited this long and worked this hard to have to also pursue and lead a man. It is not how it was meant to be.

Now some of you may have a hard time following a man. Maybe your past has shown men to not be untrustworthy or undependable. I totally get that, and it is a real thing to work through. But commit to working through it and watch what God can do with it. He can take you from not trusting and being so afraid to let someone in, to head-over-heels in love with no trace of trust issues. And God knows where you are at in the journey, and He will be gentle with you and not give you anything that you cannot handle at the time, even if it feels overwhelming and suffocating. The Holy Spirit is who you can trust, and if that person has the Holy Spirit within them as well, you will know whether you can trust them or not. This is not all on your shoulders. Let Him carry your burdens and lead you, and while you learn to follow Holy Spirit, everything will fall into place.

33.

See How Far You've Come

If you do not already journal, I highly suggest it. It doesn't have to be a "Dear Diary" type of journal, but journals are helpful when documenting your life. Journaling helps you see how far you have come and helps you evaluate your life. For instance, today I read back through a journal from three years ago. It was crazy to see how much I have grown, especially in the "being single" department. In most of my entries, I was practically begging God for my husband to magically fall into my life. Almost every entry was about that. I kept repeating myself over and over about how over it I was about being single. And here I am still single.

But now when I read journals from a year ago or less, I rarely talk about my future husband. Now I do believe it is so important to pray for your future husband and praying that he comes sooner rather than later doesn't hurt either. But there is a difference between when praying something into being and praying while whining about it. I look back, and there is such desperation and urgency in my tone. I no longer have that while I talk about it now. This is a huge feat for me considering I used to obsess over the possibility of meeting the man of my dreams. Though it is still something I desire very much so, there is not as much of a focus on it like there once was. It is so freeing to see such a huge shift.

There are down sides to journaling as well; you can also see how some things in your life haven't changed much at all. For example, externally my life looks very similar to how it looked before moving to Australia in regards to location and still figuring out what to do with my life. But who I am now internally outweighs any sort of external setbacks that others may perceive. Those things do not matter in the grand scheme of life, and the more I live, the more I learn this to be true.

Have you looked back at some of your old journal writings? If not, I encourage you to, so you can see the leaps and bounds you have made. And if you still feel like you have not grown as much as you would've liked, you can always start now. I document it through journaling, so I can share my experiences with others and never forget what I have gone through and come out of. We will never be exactly where we want to be, but when we do see how far we have come, it is encouraging and pushes us forward to get through the next hurdle.

It is important to celebrate the wins in your life because if you don't, you are just living to get by. That is you surviving and not thriving. Don't be afraid to celebrate you because that only helps others to celebrate themselves too. And the more we celebrate, the more this life of waiting is worth living and fighting for.

Change Your Language

Something I have been noticing is the way I talk about my singleness. A lot of times I make jokes about it in regards to how long I have been single. Lately I have even been having less hope about meeting my future husband and find myself making negative comments as if it will never happen. I think I am just protecting myself because there is a part of me that is afraid it will never happen and that I will be single for the rest of my life. Even though I know that is not true based on what God has spoken to me, and the desires He has put on my heart.

Earlier today I was listening to a podcast from Bethel in Redding by Bill Johnson, and he said something I have heard before, but it stood out to me like never before. He talked about having confidence in God. And it hit me; my language lately in regards to my future husband has been opposing what God has spoken and made so clear to me. If I am not having hope and speaking with confidence in God that He will bring my promise to pass and that I will get married, then it cannot happen. I mean it could because God is gracious and kind, but how much better it is if I can learn to speak with confidence from God. This is different than just regular confidence. I think in the past I have spoken in my own confidence, and hence this is why it still has not happened.

There is a will for our lives, and when we are not in tune with it, it creates internal conflict and frustration. But once we are aligned with God's will for us and speak with confidence in Him, we have nothing to worry about. You may feel silly speaking with so much hope and faith about your singleness one-day ending, but it does something in you that will shift your perspective and bring freedom.

Be careful with the words you say because they will shape your life and future. There is so much power in our words, and when we are not careful with what we say about our singleness, it can derail us or move us forward. It is our choice in what we say and how we say it. Now we don't always have to be so serious about it. I think it is great when you can laugh at yourself. That is why I joke with friends about my singleness, but there is a fine line between putting ourselves down and joking about it. The healthier the perspective we can get on being single, the better lives we can lead, single or married.

34.

Strength and Dignity

I remember a time when I was at one of my lowest. In comparison to other times in my life, I was actually not as bad. But what made it so awful is that I really did know better. I wasn't living the way I knew I should be. I knew too much about my own morals and values, but I wasn't living according to them. I thought I had been freed of so many strongholds, yet it was like they had all come back to haunt me, and I was allowing them to. One day I was on a walk by the beach in Newport Beach, California where I would go on walks often. I was listening to a podcast from Hillsong Sisterhood in Sydney, Australia where I would eventually move. The woman, who spoke, Donna Crouch, talked about when she was single. She shared that when she was twenty-nine years old, she had this revelation that she was not exactly the woman she wanted to be yet. She struggled in her singleness. And her heart's desire was to be a woman clothed in strength and dignity like it says in Proverbs 31:25. She knew she wanted to possess those qualities before she got married. And as I listened to her through my headphones, I started to cry. I too wanted that, and I had never felt so far from that.

Donna Crouch went on to tell her journey of becoming that woman *clothed in strength and dignity*. Although I do not know her personally, I have been around her while living in Australia, and she definitely exudes both of those qualities. So that too has been my journey over the last couple years. I had always considered myself a strong woman, but I was strong in the wrong sense. I was a little too rough around the edges and had some anger to deal with. But I wanted an inner strength that people could depend on; strength where I could say "no" when I needed to. Strength where I could handle any season and come out trusting God, no matter what. Dignity was harder for me than the former. I had always struggled with my worth and value. Nobility, worthiness, and self-respect define dignity. At the time, when listening to this podcast, I had very little self-respect and struggled with it for years.

But I knew it was time for me to embody these two attributes. If I could be known for anything at the end of my life, I pray that it be these two character traits. So through a lot of falling on my face and wrestling with my own weaknesses, I prayed and prayed that God would help me in these areas. I knew I was called to help empower other women to walk out in strength and dignity as well, but I needed to do it myself before I could help anyone else do it.

God slowly, but surely helped me in both of these areas. It took a lot of failing before getting it right. But He was patient and loving with me, and I am so thankful that God answered my prayers. And though He is still working on me in these two areas, and will continue for the rest of my life, I can confidently say I am a woman clothed in strength and dignity. Those two qualities have helped change my life tremendously, especially in the area of singleness. Without them, I would not be where I am today, confidently content in my singleness. With being clothed in strength and dignity comes the rest of the verse, "and she laughs without fear of the future." As we rise up and embody strength and dignity, we no longer need to be worried about whom we will marry, when we will get married, and how it will all happen. We no longer make wrong choices that end up hurting us in the long run. Focus on those two things in your life and watch God's peace fill your heart so full that you can laugh at what is to come because you know that it will be so much better than anything you could have ever imagined. So start laughing a joyful, bold and confident laughter because He is faithful, and you have nothing to fear.

Strength and dignity are keys that will unlock so much potential in your life. Not only will they give you the potential to being an amazing girlfriend and eventually wife, they will change the way in which you carry yourself. People will look to you as an example. There is nothing more attractive than someone who can hold their head up high and not apologize for who they are. Someone who does not worry about what is ahead, but instead stands firm in what they believe and waits for God to act on their behalf, now that is what faith looks like. Even nonbelievers can appreciate faith like that. This is our purpose as women, to be the kind of person who does not back down or worry about the future because they trust in a God who knows the beginning to the end and the end to the beginning.

Know Your Value and Worth

I have said it before, and I will say it again: know your value and worth. Stop looking for it in others or in what you do. The only way you will fully understand how valuable and worthy you are is by finding it within Jesus Christ and yourself. Forget about old experiences, negative words that were spoken over you, and start grabbing hold of truth. Find truth in the Word of God and through prayer. Sit and let the Holy Spirit speak to you. This may sound weird and crazy to you, depending on where you are at on your spiritual journey. But I promise, if you practice it and are consistent in sitting and waiting to hear from God, He will eventually speak to you. You may hear an audible voice or you may get a small nudge or thought that comes out of nowhere, and that is the Holy Spirit speaking to you.

You may have been like me and grew up in a negative and hostile environment where you didn't get the validation and encouragement you needed. But that does not mean you can't get that now. It does not mean you have to live like that anymore. You can choose a different, better life if you are willing to be dedicated to not settling in any area of life and if you want it badly enough that you are willing to surrender everything (mind, body and soul) over to Jesus. You may ask yourself *how do I do that*. All you need to do is tell God you want what He has for you and you want to change and mean it from the bottom of your heart, genuinely; and He will be faithful and will make it happen slowly but surely.

It makes me so sad to think about how many women don't know how valued they are by their Heavenly Father. I used to be one of them, so I understand. It is hard to know and believe it when the rest of the world tells you the opposite. But to God, we are His royal daughters, worthy of love, respect and honor. There are two worlds that surround us at all times, the physical world and the spiritual. God operates out of the spiritual world, and everything there is opposite to how it is here on earth. It is a hard thing to grasp. But when we start living out of the spiritual in the physical, the miraculous can take place.

Your past may tell you one thing, but God is telling you another. When we receive His love for us that can only be found through knowing our intrinsic value, then we are able to live fulfilled and purposeful lives. This is how God intended it. If you have struggled with not feeling good enough at any point in your life, I am sorry that you have felt that way. I have been there, and it is one of the worst feelings. But let me tell you from someone who now has the revelation of how worthy and valued I am, there is a better way of living and you don't have to feel like that any longer. Jesus will set you free if you let Him. Again, it is a choice. He gives us free will, so we can choose what we want in life rather than having a God who just controls our every step. No, He wants more for us. This beautiful life full of His goodness and faithfulness is available for each and every one of us.

Then when we get our value from the source of Truth, we are able to have better relationships. When we do not put pressure on others to tell us who we are and show us our value, it gives room for authentic relationships that are not strained by unnecessary expectations. It is no one else's job to complete us other than God's. Many times relationships and marriages fail because one or both people are looking to the other to complete them and fulfill them when no one can do that other than Jesus.

When you start knowing your worth and value, everything starts changing around you. You start attracting the right things into your life, the right people, the right opportunities, the right relationships. You become confident and are not phased by things you once were torn apart by. The grass stops looking greener on the other side. You start appreciating what you have and the things in your life. But this really can only be done when we are connected to the Father and understand we are His daughters. But if you ask Him, He will show you how just like anything in life. Your relationship with Him is your most powerful tool for changing how you view yourself and how others view you. It is a big risk, but it is well worth it when you start seeing the progress and growth in and around you.

The Single Sisterhood

If we are going to be single, meaning we are alone, why not be alone together? Singleness which is oftentimes looked at as not ideal should become a cool club. It's like when couples become friends with other couples and then never invite their single friends to things. Well we should have a singles only club called *the Single Sisterhood.*

Ok, I am totally joking. Some of you may have thought that was a great idea, which I am not totally opposed to. But what I will say is we should stick together. Single girls unite because we really need each other. No one understands better the frustrations and annoying days of singleness like another single girl. I mean we have our friends who were once single, but they don't get it anymore. They found their *Prince Charming.* They no longer remember the horrible dating scene or if they do, they try to forget it. They no longer get how difficult it is to find a guy you are attracted to and actually enjoy talking to. For some reason it is so hard to find one guy with even just those two things going for him. And it is nothing against those guys, I mean for someone else they would be perfect, but for you- no, there is just nothing there. And that is okay! You aren't going to click with everyone.

But seriously, who knows better than another single girl? We need to stick together if we are going to get through this. Sometimes we need an understanding shoulder to cry on. Or we need a friend who doesn't judge us for eating that tub of Ben and Jerry's all to ourselves while we watch The Notebook and cry the majority of the movie. It no longer is about the movie, but somehow the movie has become about us and our pitiful lives. See, once a girl makes it out of *The Single Sisterhood,* she somehow gets amnesia and forgets that she ever had that life. She forgets the terrible times, the nights of crying herself to sleep, as she now lays next to her hot husband in marital bliss after a long evening of sex. While the single girl lies alone; no one to even cuddle or kiss goodnight. We don't even need the sex yet which obviously would be very helpful and enjoyable every now and again, but at this point we would be good with just a hand to hold. This is when you know you are as single as it gets.

Now I know marriage isn't going to be one nonstop sex-fest or this romantic, beautiful experience every day or even every week, month, or year. I have enough married friends nowadays to know and see that it isn't as exciting as I may have built it up in my head at times. And most of the time, it is no lovemaking scene from *The Notebook.* But I still beg to differ, that it is in fact pretty awesome. And I still hold firm to the fact that I would rather be hugging a man then my pillow at night. I would still rather be able to have the option of having sex. And I would still rather fight with someone than fight by myself. If you are single and understand what I mean, can I get an Amen? Amen!

We know the drill, we understand what marriage is and isn't. And we won't fully get it until we are married. But until then, I would rather think it is more beautiful and special than it may actually be because at least it gives me something to look forward to after I have endured these many years of singleness where I have so looked forward to the day when I finally get to say "I do." So let us not burst our own idealized marital bubble and stick together girls.

The Single Sisterhood, our new club, needs to not only stick together, but we need to pray together. Pray for your single friends. Pray for their future husbands and families. Pray for peace and comfort or whatever your single sister needs. Encourage one another in your times of singleness. Don't leave anyone to fend for themself. It helps so much when you can have a band of incredible women who are on the same page and stage as you. So face this time with your girls, make it fun and enjoyable. Be careful not to have a *bitchfest* too often about how much it sucks being single because that doesn't get anyone anywhere. If one of your girls keeps being negative, remind them of hope and joy. Remind them to keep focused on all the good that singleness can be. But it is okay to laugh at yourselves and not take anything too seriously. It can definitely be a very challenging time, but it too can be fun and freeing.

35.

Spring is Here

Earlier in this book I wrote about my long winter season where I have been waiting for God to do something amazing in my life. And what I have found is that spring is all around. Spring can be found in your winter season if you are looking for it. I would say in some areas of my life I am still in a winter season where I am waiting for certain things to happen. I am waiting for my life to "take off" in different areas. But personally and spiritually, I am in a spring season. God is using me, some days more than others. He is speaking to me and showing me things, again some days more than others. But what is important is that He is there. I can find spring when I create that time and space for it. Spring flowers make me forget about the cold winter I may be facing in some areas of my life. Life is filled with seasons, and I believe you can have a season within a season. Winter doesn't always have to be so hard to endure; it can be embraced, and some snow can melt for the day with some sun peeking through.

Currently, I am still waiting on a lot of things to happen in my life. A good job where I can support myself and actually save. I am waiting for a relationship with the man of my prayers. But with saying that, so many things have taken place that I can boast in the Lord about. I have a small home to myself, an answer to prayer. God has already helped me grow so much in my confidence in who He has created me to be these last few months. He has shown me love like I have never known. He is teaching me more and more how to hear from Him. He has blessed me with a couple trips the last few months. I no longer stress like I once had about how I am going to live when I have very little income. He is taking care of me in this winter season. And those blessings, I call spring. All throughout our lives we will have these seasons within seasons if we let them filter in. God can only bless us if we are open to His blessings. How I have allowed Him to is by being grateful for what I do have and praising Him when I don't feel like it. When we worship Him through the good and bad, it puts things into perspective.

I could sit here and wallow in self-pity over the fact that I STILL am single and I STILL am struggling financially at the ripe old age of twenty-eight (I'm being sarcastic of course). But honestly, sometimes I want to feel sorry for myself when many around me are way further along in those areas. But an area that I am further along in, generally speaking, is my growth and strength through my relationship with God. I have gumption and not many people can say that about themselves. I know the only way I got there is by enduring some hard, cold winter seasons when I could have avoided them. But instead I pressed in and didn't give up. And I am reaping the benefits of that now.

My Happily Ever After

When I first decided to start taking writing seriously and write this book, I was hoping it would have a different ending. My idea was that I would take you through my own personal journey and struggles as well as a few of my friends, and by the end of the book; I would have met my future husband. I thought how great it would be to write about being single, and the very last chapter I would tell you about my happily ever after. I was going to tell you about how we met and the process of us starting to date. He was going to be a dream and say the nicest things. He was going to treat me like a princess, and all of my theories, thoughts, and opinions I previously wrote about were going to come true.

Unfortunately my plans did not pan out. But do things ever really go the way we planned? In my experience, that has not really been the case, hence me still being single. But you know what, I may not have had my fairytale ending yet. I may still be waiting for *Mr. Right* to walk on by, but I can honestly say I am happy. I am happy being single, for now of course. I am happy because I am confident in who I am. I no longer look for approval from men. I no longer waste my time and emotions on guys who aren't worth it. Am I tempted to at times still? You bet! But I don't give in like I used to. I am content in being single because I love who I am and I know the person I end up with will love who I am too. And I will love him.

Being single for this long has been one of the greatest gifts in my life. God has used this time to shape me into the woman He needed me to be before getting married. God used this time to help me fall in love with Him and trust Him with my whole heart before anyone else gets my heart. He has shown me how special I am and did not want to just give me to anyone. The man who God has for me is remarkable and has had his own journey of getting there. We both haven't been ready to meet each other and that is okay because I would rather do some deep, hard work now rather than even harder, messier work later with someone else involved.

I would love it if I could tell you that this book works, just look at my life. But unfortunately meeting your future husband is not a formula to be followed. There is no right or wrong way of doing things. It is full of ups and downs with some twist and turns.

All we can do is learn from our own and others' experiences and mistakes and be the best version of ourselves we can be. I may have to wait five more years before I get married (God willing, that won't be the case). But even if I do have to wait five or ten or twenty more years, I can honestly say I would wait if it was what God wanted me to do and if that meant I would get to marry the man who is intended to be my husband. I never in a million years thought I would ever say something like that. I used to say, *if I don't have a boyfriend by the time I am eighteen I will DIE* (in a very dramatic, teenage voice). But here I am, ten years later, and I am still alive. I am not only alive, but I am ALIVE. I live with purpose, more than just looking to be married, but a purpose that is rooted deeply in me that is greater than just getting married and being a wife, which is a beautiful purpose, but we are called to that and so much more.

God desires each of His daughters to walk in strength and dignity. He calls us royalty, and once we understand that and live out of that, we can then be treated like the princesses we are by our own *Prince Charming*. I know that my time is coming soon to meet the love of my life. I have to believe that and hold onto it because my Heavenly Father promised me. And until it is my time, I will continue to learn and grow like I have these last few years I shared with you. I hope to tell you all about him very soon!

Now What

We are at the end of our journey together as two single girls hoping and waiting for the man of our dreams. While we wait we have much to do, much to look forward to, and much to enjoy. We have worked on letting go of our past, forgiving who we need to forgive. We have let God take us through the wilderness, in our lonely seasons. We have learned to love ourselves and not get carried away with ideals that are not helpful. We have learned to be strong and have dignity. We now know our value and who we are. We no longer look to men for our identity. On our journey we have let people help us when we need help. As we continue on this road of singleness, we now understand that it will not last forever, and it is a gift.

I hope you have learned some of these things while reading some of my story. I hope that my mistakes, heartaches, and adventures have helped you see that you are not alone in this. My prayer is that you will be set free and that you genuinely do love being single during times of this season because this single season won't last forever. It can be done in such a way that causes you to become a stronger, more beautiful and confident you. Remember that singleness is not a punishment and that there is nothing you can do or not do that will help you out of it. The way out is simply God's grace and timing. When it is your time to be joined with your future husband, God will make it happen, regardless of any other factors. Your mistakes were not for nothing, and God always uses everything for good.

You may find yourself still struggling in your singleness after reading this. This book is not magic, but I do believe and pray it will bring miracles into your life whether that is through *Mr. Right* walking into your life or you finding yourself content in your singleness. But even more so, I pray for miracles that will transform you from the inside. I pray that strongholds will be broken and old ways of thinking would be gone. I pray that you truly know how valuable and precious you are, and no man can take that away from you, or give it to you either - except for one man, Jesus Christ. You may not be a Jesus follower but still read these pages filled with His goodness because deep down you long for something more than you have yet to experience. You are not alone in that. Even some Jesus followers have yet to experience the unconditional love He has for them. Lover of Jesus or not, He waits to heal your broken heart and comfort you through all seasons of life. If you want to receive Jesus Christ as your Lord and Savior, simply ask him. Pray and ask Jesus into your heart and to be your first love. He is waiting for you.

With everything we have discussed and covered in these pages, you are probably wondering…now what? I'm still single.

You are still single. Why did I even read this? And I hope you aren't thinking those things, but in case you are, please be patient. Be patient and wait for the right man. Please do not sell yourself short and date a bunch of guys you don't even really like. Please don't waste your time on any guy who doesn't pursue you the way you would like him to. Choose to remain single over settling because those sacrifices now of waiting, will pay off in the long run.

These days, marriages barely last - the divorce rate is high. I even know couples who are around my age who have already been divorced. It is heartbreaking and sad, but it doesn't have to be us. If we prepare ourselves now while we still can, commit to growing and transforming into who we are meant to be, the rest of it will fall into place. We do not need to worry or try to manipulate our lives or any guys' to try and make something happen. At the perfect time and with the perfect guy for you, a miracle can take place, and you will no longer be single but moving into the next season of life. There will still be challenges there, the grass isn't always greener, but it will be promises fulfilled, loving and beautiful memories made. The highs and the lows will no longer be done on your own, but you will have a life partner to take on challenges with.

Until the day you move past being single and become part of a duo - apply these principles to your life and learn to trust while you wait. And when you do become part of a couple, continue to do these things and even more. God will help you along the way if you let Him. And if you make a few mistakes, which you will, let them go and learn from them. That is all we can do. I am believing and praying for your future husband, and even more so your single season to be full of contentment.

Love always,
Kirston xx

Acknowledgments

Thank you to all my friends and family for supporting and encouraging me to write this book. Thank you to everyone who would ask me when it was coming out. At times this was frustrating to me, only because I didn't have an answer most of the time, but you reminded me of what was on my heart and that propelled me to finish this book.

Thank you to all the guys I have dated, been confused by, and wished things would have worked out. Even more so I am grateful to the men who have not confused me, who have been clear with their intentions; though we were not meant to be, you taught me a lot, and I hope and pray for the very best for you.

All the tears I have cried, lonely nights, fun times, and girl chats have all been worth it because it has brought me here. I have had the privilege to share my heart with whoever has chosen to read this labor of love. You have been a part of my dream come true.

For more of Kirston's thoughts and work, ways to connect, and future endeavors please visit wild-flower.org and follow @wild.flowermedia on Instagram.

Resources

2. The Meantime: To Date or Not to Date?

Page 11 *"a 33% higher risk"*: "Does Premarital Cohabitation Raise Your Risk of Divorce?" *Council on Contemporary Families*, 1 Mar. 2014, contemporaryfamilies.org/cohabitation-divorce-brief-report/.

4. Letting It Go: Learning To Let Go

Page 26 Book referenced: Voskamp, Ann. One Thousand Gifts: a Dare to Live Fully Right Where You Are. Zondervan, 2015.

16. Limitless

Page 101 "Imagine yourself as a living house…": *Lewis, C. S. Mere Christianity: the Case for Christianity, Christian Behaviour, and beyond Personality. HarperCollins, 1998.*

17. Is It Love?: Fast Break

Page 111 Book referenced: Franklin, Jentezen. *Fasting*. Charisma House, 2014.

32. It Happens Out of No Where: We Need Validation

Page 204 Book referenced: Chapman, Gary D. The Five Love Languages: *the Secrete to Love That Last*. Christian Art Publishers, 2017.